# HERBERT VON KARAJAN
## A Life in Pictures

Published in the United States and Canada in 2007 by Amadeus Press
An Imprint of Hal Leonard Corporation
19 West 21st Street
New York, NY 10019
USA

First published in France in 2007

Design: Verlhac Editions

An original Verlhac Editions creation

Verlhac Editions
41 rue d'Artois 75008 Paris - France
www.verlhaceditions.com

Library of Congress Cataloging-in-Publication Data available.

ISBN-10: 1574671650
ISBN-13: 9781574671650

Printed in Germany in October 2007

Translated by Isabel Cole

www.amadeuspress.com

Cover picture: Siegfried Lauterwasser

# HERBERT VON KARAJAN
## A Life in Pictures
Edited by Pierre-Henri Verlhac

# FOREWORD

By Anne-Sophie Mutter

December 11, 1976, a damp, grey Saturday in Berlin: to this day I remember the butterflies in my stomach and the burning desire to be anywhere but auditioning for Herbert von Karajan right now. He had previously suggested an appointment in August – but first I had fled on vacation, a modest and useless attempt to put off the day of truth forever.

Years before I had used my allowance to buy my first record – Bruckner's Symphony No. 4 with Herbert von Karajan and the Berlin Philharmonic. The recording shook me to my very foundations: never before had I heard such beauty of tone and such fascinating arcs of tension. How could I possibly live up to the demands of this brilliant conductor? Disaster seemed inevitable.

I was ushered into the conductor's room to find a man at great pains to relieve me of all my tension and fear. His aura alone would have made me forget all my reservations instantly. Herbert von Karajan requested Bach's Chaconne – saying that due to time pressures, however, he could not listen to the entire, twenty-minute work. In the end, the audition included not only the entire Chaconne, but two movements of a Mozart violin concerto as well. Then, as I put away my violin, Herbert von Karajan turned to my teacher, Aida Stucki, and left the room. On the way back into the concert hall the maestro came up to me and said: "I'm looking forward to our Whitsun concert next year in Salzburg." The Philharmonic trembled under my feet.

That day was the beginning of a musical collaboration whose intensity has never been matched for me. It brought with it a very special honor, for in these thirteen years up to his death I was his only violin soloist – in the concert hall and the recording studio. Fortunately, however, I was not his only protegee, for here too Herbert von Karajan set standards: to this day no other musician has smoothed the way to an international stage career for so many colleagues, be they singers, instrumentalists or conductors.

Herbert von Karajan will always be a role model for me. With his implacable discipline at rehearsals and his permanent engagement with the composition, he achieved total freedom and authority on the evening of the concert. He taught me that even the smallest detail of the score carries immense significance. Karajan's great humility before the musical work can also be seen in the fact that he refrained from performing and recording certain compositions of the Viennese Classic until his last creative period, as with the recording of Bruckner's 7th Symphony with the Vienna Philharmonic in April 1989.

And what about contemporary music? Here too Herbert von Karajan was incredibly open-minded and not at all set in his opinions. He was always happy to learn something new. And thus he was also interested in the musical projects I had established outside his sphere of influence. One of our last artistic plans– aside from the Berg violin concerto – was to perform Lutoslawski's *Chain 2*.

The same insatiable thirst for knowledge and curiosity about the future must have motivated Karajan to capture his artistic activities in a wide range of media – to the great benefit of the entire classical music community. He played a pioneering role as a meticulous innovator of recording technology and in his use of visual media for presenting music.

To this day, Herbert von Karajan remains the embodiment of classical music all around the world. His omnipresence in the media was also held against him – by those who did not understand what his aim was. Karajan's goal in life was to take music around the globe without having to market his personal life. The publicity photos showing him with fast cars, a yacht or a jet gave the superficial viewer the illusion of a private intimacy which Karajan never allowed the audience. He was a master at this balancing act, avoiding scandals and embarrassments without catering to the masses as a media character. Since his death classical music has lost a broad public space that is now occupied by the mainstream and a deluge of industrial culture productions. By contrast, Herbert von Karajan's standards of quality shine timelessly as a lodestar in the musical firmament.

# HERBERT VON KARAJAN LEGEND AND (MUSICAL) LEADER

by Jürgen Otten

The anecdote is fictitious, but telling. Leonard Bernstein, Karl Böhm and Herbert von Karajan are sitting around discussing which conductor is the greatest. Böhm says: "I'm the greatest." Bernstein contradicts him: he, Bernstein, is the greatest. Böhm asks Bernstein who told him that. Bernstein, with an ecstatic gleam in his eyes: "God told me that." At that moment Karajan interrupts: "I never said anything of the kind."

Sometimes a few clever words contain more truth than whole volumes. And no one would seriously dispute that Herbert von Karajan is a legend, one created by himself and others. A mere selection of the epithets devised for the artist serves as proof: "miracle", "phenomenon", "myth", "the almighty", "maestrissimo", "magician", "the Pope of music", "Omnifex maximus" – all these imaginative locutions are based on the same principle: what one fails to grasp is couched in something emblematic that expresses this very failure. The sacrosanct nature of the object is, as it were, the fundamental prerequisite for the engagement with an ambivalent personality; this can be seen in the religious connotations of some of these epithets.

Perhaps the most apt characterization comes from the musical sociologist Theodor W. Adorno, who called Karajan the "genius of the economic miracle". This points to a central ambivalence in Karajan's life and creative-interpretive work: the genius is a child of the nineteenth century, a child of Romanticism whose raison d'être was called into question with increasing vehemence over the course of the twentieth century. The concept of the genius was replaced by the belief in collective progress and by unstoppable economic and technological development, a context in which the work of art alters as well. This antagonism took prominent form in Herbert von Karajan, the Catholic son of the city of Salzburg. Karajan fused the genius with the belief in progress. Not merely in an artistic sense: his very being and actions melded ecstasy and control, pathos and poetry, passion and perfection. Karajan was traditionalist and modernist in one; his interpretive style was a synthesis of his much-admired "demigods", of Furtwängler's imagination and Toscanini's will to precision. Günter Grass called Karajan "a perfect child". Walter Benjamin anticipated his inscrutable charisma when he defined aura as "the unique phenomenon of a distance however close it may be". To this day Karajan's inapproachability has remained a central quality of his cult image. And if ever anyone embodied Canetti's saying that the conductor is the ruler of the world as long as the world consists of nothing but the work, it was Herbert von Karajan. This was due not least to an immense output of effort. Hardly a conductor rehearsed so intensively, none devoted himself so obsessively to the perusal of the score – Karajan actually knew by heart all the scores he conducted.

The complexity of his personality was beautifully captured by Wolfgang Stresemann, who worked at his side for decades as the director of the Berlin Philharmonic: "Karajan is like the weather. Both are a constant topic of conversation, though one can't do anything about them. Both are unpredictable. There is an eternal guessing-game about Karajan as a person. He too is a person with his contradictions, contrasts, inconsistencies, a person who both attracts and repels, always at the center of violent controversies. Charming and likeable when he wants to be, rarely warm, usually somewhat distant, often cool and standoffish, even intentionally wounding to a painful degree. He knows all this, and at the same time he doesn't know it. He is quite capable of being his own harshest critic, also in the assessment of his concerts; sometimes he judges other people – musicians and non-musicians – hastily and superficially, rarely listening when one tries to amend his judgment. Incidentally, he is a poor judge of people, insecure in this respect as well, filled with such a profound, dominant mistrust that one is led to believe he mistrusts himself."

## A Knight's Apprenticeship

Karajan was a Sunday child. He first saw the light of day on April 5, 1908, in Salzburg, the second son of the respected senior physician Ernst von Karajan and his wife, Martha. In the baptismal register he is listed as Sir Heribert von Karajan. The family's forebears came from the border region between Greece and Macedonia. The title von was first given to the merchant Georg Johann in the second half of the eighteenth century. From then on the family embarked on a continuous rise through society.

Sir Heribert was a sickly boy. It is quite possible that the roots of his lifelong, indomitable ambition lie here. "I always had to see to it that I went further than the others," Karajan was to say in his old age, looking back. And the penchant for perfection in all he undertook was already pronounced at this early age. Hating everything dilettantish, Heribert always demanded the best, the utmost – of himself and of others. Music quickly acquired a dominant role in the life of the little knight. Two pianos and a harmonium stood in the house, and not just as decoration. The boy practiced as much as four hours a day. His father, Ernst, could also be found at the piano – when his scant time permitted, and when he was not busy "tootling" on his favorite instrument, the clarinet. In a delightful Sunday ritual, two aunts came to perform little pieces "with rachitic fingers" (Karajan). It was always too slow for the boy. Even then his inner tempo was faster. But he also had difficulties with his hands. "I wanted to have a career as a pianist," he told the biographer Roger Vaughan, "but there was just one problem: the tendons of my fingers are not anatomically

perfect; they become inflamed very easily. That meant that I had to take a break from time to time."

At the tender age of four years Heribert heard the prelude to Wagner's opera *The Mastersingers of Nuremberg* and the first act of *The Valkyrie*, and began taking his first piano lessons with Franz Ledwinka. One year later he made his official debut. In a hotel near Salzburg he interpreted a rondo by Mozart. The auditorium was captivated. What great talent! But was the performer a wunderkind? Karajan himself always denied it. And over the course of his career he repeatedly emphasized that he had always had difficulties. Miracles have a different sound.

From 1917 to 1926 Heribert studied at the Salzburg Mozarteum. He continued to study piano with Ledwinka, making great progress: at the age of sixteen he had mastered such challenging works as Liszt's First Piano Concerto. In addition, he took classes in the subjects of harmonics, music history, composition and chamber music. Heribert's teacher in the latter two subjects was Bernhard Paumgartner, director of the Mozarteum: a moderately gifted conductor and author of a Mozart biography. Paumgartner directed the boy's passion toward conducting, initially with only modest success. The fascination of the piano was still greater than that of the baton. A benevolent appraisal of a performance in the Mozarteum characterized the boy's interpretation of Mozart's Fantasia in D minor as performed "calmly and confidently from memory, unconscious of the abysses and lurking dangers, graceful and animated."

The year 1920 brought changes, fundamental ones. The Salzburg Festival was founded, run by the trio of Hugo von Hofmannsthal, Richard Strauss and Max Reinhardt, with Paumgartner brought on board as musical adviser. The young Karajan's passion for theater was awakened; never again was he to leave this magical artistic realm. He participated in the Festival first as a choirboy, then as rehearser and Bühnenkapellmeister. Not only did he hear his first full-length opera there (*The Valkyrie*), he also came into contact with Arturo Toscanini. Not personally – Sir Heribert was too shy for that. But he experienced the important artist at close range. He heard Verdi's *Falstaff* – which Toscanini conducted in Salzburg and then in Vienna – forty-six times, including rehearsals. Decades later Karajan declared that this had been "my life's most staggering impression", but not the only one: "I have Toscanini to thank for a special experience. That was when he came to Vienna with La Scala to do *Lucia di Lammermoor*. Lucia was actually frowned upon in Vienna at the time. As young people we asked ourselves how someone could even choose this 'organ grinder's music'. It took just five minutes to completely change our minds. At the time something awoke inside me, and I have cultivated it ever since. I became convinced that there is no such thing as 'hackneyed music'. It only becomes hackneyed when you make it that way."

### I Got It

In 1927, having pocketed the school leaving examination along with the Mozarteum diploma, the nineteen-year-old Karajan left Salzburg, abandoning both the "Sir" and the "i" in his first name. In Vienna he enrolled in the Technical College – but not without continuing to perfect himself as a pianist. His teacher was Josef Hofmann, namesake of the legendary Polish-American pianist. The scales soon tipped. Someone who intends to practice for eight hours a day cannot deal with engineering questions on top of that. After three semesters Karajan left the Technical College for good. From then on he attended musical lectures at the University, hurried to the opera or the theater whenever possible and devoted the rest of his time to his piano lessons; even then he avoided convivial evenings. Unfortunately, success was not quick in materializing. On the contrary; carpal tunnel syndrome thwarted the ambitious pupil's expectations. But all was not lost. Karajan turned to the third option for becoming a man of importance – conducting. The only problem was that there were no qualified teachers at the Academy of Music and Performing Arts. Clemens Krauss had just given up the directorship of the conducting class in order to become the director of the Vienna State Opera. He was replaced by the oboist of the Vienna Philharmonic, Alexander Wunderer. Herbert von Karajan's first appearance as a conductor came in Wunderer's "term of office". On December 17, 1928, he conducted the Academy's student orchestra in the closing concert of Wunderer's conducting class. And he was interested in just one thing: the one piece that evening that eschewed soloists, giving the conductor the best possible chance to distinguish himself (in front of the others as well) – Rossini's William Tell Overture. Later Karajan remembered vividly: "I took it into my head that I had to get this piece. Back then, when I wanted something, I withdrew for days, preparing myself and concentrating. – I got it." It was not the last time that he would be in a position to say these words.

Spurred on by his triumph, he arranged his next coup with the help of friends. On January 22, 1929, Karajan conducted the Mozarteum Orchestra in Salzburg with a stellar program: Mozart's A Major Piano Concerto, KV 488, Tchaikovsky's Fifth Symphony, and finally Strauss' symphonic poem Don Juan, the work that would come to stand paradigmatically for his future role as conqueror of the musical world. In the audience was a man who could hardly believe his eyes and ears and was willing to serve as Karajan's accomplice: Erwin Dietrich, the artistic director of the Ulm Municipal Theater. Right

after the concert he offered Karajan a trial engagement as Second Kapellmeister at his theater. Karajan, who had never before conducted a work for the stage, agreed on one condition: he wanted to produce an entire opera. Dietrich gulped, then gave his blessing – and placed the new production of Mozart's Le nozze di Figaro in Karajan's hands.

It is hard to imagine a bolder beginning. When Karajan arrived in Ulm in January 1929, he was met by an orchestra consisting of seventeen musicians who were anything but highly skilled. And Germany's oldest theater, with 600 seats, was in a desolate state. But Karajan was not the man to let that trouble him. He plunged into his work with élan; after all, the premiere was not quite six weeks away. The effort paid off. Figaro was a triumph – and Karajan was engaged as Kapellmeister until the following summer. He was to stay in Ulm for five seasons in total, thus experiencing something that many conductors, but few of the great ones, have gone through: the "salt mines", with little pay and lots of work. His salary came to a modest eighty marks, and a premiere was scheduled every two weeks. Karajan slaved away day in, day out, with the orchestra, with the singers; at night he studied the scores. He was bothered by the mediocrity that pervaded every artistic area, but he bore with it in order to be forearmed for the future. For instance, there was no adequate cast for the Mastersingers, and the stage was just barely six and a half yards wide – yet he conducted Wagner's difficult opera twelve times in a row. When Karajan stepped up to the podium at the Bayreuth Festival in 1951 to perform the same work, he knew the score back to front; he had also performed the Mastersingers in Aachen in 1935 and in Berlin in 1939. The aggregate result was a supreme artistic essence. For this and other reasons Karajan would later look back approvingly on the years of his apprenticeship: "An artistic career must be built slowly and arduously – it takes half one's life." Karajan was lucky: for him it would take only twenty years before he could knock at the gates of Olympus.

### Germany's Youngest Generalmusikdirektor

Returning to the year 1934, Karajan's work contract in Ulm was terminated against his will. His departure in March highlighted the drama of the situation: he conducted the new staging of Le nozze di Figaro – the work with which he had debuted in Ulm. Suddenly he was on the street, without work, without a future. Once again Karajan was forced to struggle. Based in Berlin, he spent half a year crisscrossing the German Reich by train in search of a suitable job. Nothing but disappointments. Then, unexpectedly, a glimmer of hope. In Berlin he met the artistic director of the Aachen Theater, Edgar Gross, who was willing to give him a hearing. Politically speaking, Gross was no tabula rasa: member of the NSDAP, paying member of the SS and member of the Nazi Air Corps. This was not without significance for Karajan; with Aachen's previous Generalmusikdirektor Peter Raabe named successor to Richard Strauss as President of the Reich Chamber of Music, theater director Gross was in search of a new First Kapellmeister capable of representing the glory of Germanic culture on the Reich's western border. Karajan struck him as suitable, but when he auditioned the orchestra objected. Too fiery, too demanding. Gross asserted himself and engaged the exceptional talent.

At the beginning of his tenure in late summer 1934 Karajan conducted Beethoven's *Fidelio*. The audience was beside itself, the critics no less so. After that things came thick and fast. Karajan chose cleverly, conducting works he had in his repertoire such as *Rosenkavalier*, *Tannhäuser* and Händel's *Julius Caesar*, trying out some new things such as *The Magic Flute, The Valkyrie* and *Siegfried*, and making a successful foray into concert conducting. The musicians had long since grasped that Karajan was capable of taking them to unprecedented heights. Sensing this himself, he soon demanded still more. And by 1935 the twenty seven-year-old Herbert von Karajan had become Germany's youngest Generalmusikdirektor, provided not only with the control of the opera, but of the Municipal Orchestra as well, not to mention a three-year contract and a respectable income of 14,000 marks.

Was all well, then? Unfortunately not. For Herbert von Karajan made a mistake; whether knowingly or not is beside the point. Until the end of his life Karajan was repeatedly confronted with the question of why he entered the NSDAP not just once, but twice. This is how he described the incident to his biographer, Ernst Haeussermann: "It's no secret, I was a party member; I joined in 1935 in Aachen when I was to become Generalmusikdirektor. Three days before my appointment, with the longed-for goal in front of me, the city director came to me and said: 'Listen, there's' – and these were his words: 'there's one more formality to take care of. You're not a party member yet. According to the NSDAP circuit leader, however, you can't hold a post of this kind without being a party member.' So I signed."

Many have called this version into question, chiefly Fred K. Prieberg, author of the book *Musik im NS-Staat*. The fact of the matter is: back when Karajan was Kapellmeister in Ulm, he had already let a Salzburg friend of the family, party member Herbert Klein, recruit him for the NSDAP – on his twenty fifth birthday, of all things. His membership number was 1607525. The reasons for his enrollment in the party are obscure; Karajan himself never shed any light on them. The most probable explanation is that he let Klein per-suade him and then forgot the matter. Even at that time politics did not interest him. No dues payments by Karajan following that April 1933 have been recorded; thus, his enrollment had remained without consequences. His second, actual admittance to the party took place in April of 1935; his membership number was 3430914.

Certainly this was no praiseworthy behavior on Karajan's part. But in the face of the moral outrage that has lasted to this day, it is worth citing a dissenting voice. And who better than a certain Herbert Frahm. Frahm, who fought against the Nazis in Scandinavia under the cover name Willy Brandt, came to the following conclusion in his memoirs – referring specifically to Furtwängler, but ultimately including Karajan as well: "Later generations that accuse the conductor of having served the Nazis do not know what they are talking about. The paths between exceptional art and disgraceful politics are complex."

Biographer Karl Löbl also recognized the primacy of career over political consciousness: "He joined. Without reservations. His professional career was the most important thing for him. He did not identify with the regime. Like so many other artists, he was completely indifferent, politically speaking." So indifferent that in October 1942 he would marry Anna Maria Gütermann. According to the Nazis' racial laws, the attractive young woman was a "quarter-Jew".

**A Decidedly Modern Conductor**

On April 8, 1938, Karajan made his debut with the orchestra he had first experienced eleven years before in Salzburg under the direction of Wilhelm Furtwängler: he conducted the Berlin Philharmonic. The only word to describe the program is "bold": Mozart's youthfully fresh Symphony in B Major, KV 319, Ravel's second *Daphnis et Chloé Suite* and Brahms' Fourth. The gamble paid off. The review by the Swiss composer and journalist Robert Oboussier in the Deutsche Allgemeine Zeitung was little short of prophetic. He wrote, in rather bombastic diction: "The accomplishment of the evening hit almost like a bomb [...] Karajan is a decidedly modern conductor. He seeks the clear structure of a rigorous, self-contained form. But this rendering of form at an austere distance from the self is suffused by the passion of surrender to the work. In the blossoming sound, intellect and sensuality interpenetrate one another in the loveliest equilibrium". Overlooking the piece's expressionist coloring, one has a description of the typical Karajan style that was to assert itself over the following decades. On September 30 Karajan stood on the podium with the Philharmonic once again, at a Kraft durch Freude master concert with symphonies by Sibelius and Beethoven. Soon after that he was put through the wringer of Nazi cultural policy.

The background was a turf battle between the two men who controlled the fate of Berlin's cultural institutions at that time: on the one hand Hermann Göring, Prussian Minister President (among other things), on the other Joseph Goebbels, head of the Propaganda Ministry. Goebbels wanted to bring the rebellious Furtwängler into line, and he knew that the easiest way to go about it was to install a serious competitor. Karajan, who had recently married the attractive Aachen opera singer Elmy Holgerloef, fit into his plans perfectly. On the very same day the fate of Czechoslovakia was sealed in Munich, he directed *Fidelio* at the State Opera. At one of the few rehearsals, general manager Heinz Tietjen introduced him to Gustav Gründgens, who was frantically seeking a Kapellmeister for his new production of *The Magic Flute*. Karajan agreed and conducted the premiere in December 1938. The cooperation with Gründgens functioned beautifully; the director proved to be a highly musical person. Later Karajan recalled this *Magic Flute*, whose overture, incidentally, was to become the first of his approximately 800 recordings: "Gründgen's staging would still be valid today. Unfortunately, many of its truths have been forgotten [...] For my own productions, it taught me that one can never actually depict a person's essence. It is always voiced by the others. The same thing is true in *Don Giovanni*. The others talk about him. Therein lies his greatness."

### The Tristan Incident

On October 21, three weeks after his triumph with *Fidelio*, Karajan conducted Wagner's masterpiece *Tristan and Isolde* at a repertory performance. And, believe it or not, he conducted the opera, which he had quite successfully debuted on June 1, 1937 at the Vienna State Opera, without a score, and that even in the rehearsals. A bold venture – and a successful one. The performance ended with ovations. The next day the *B.Z. am Mittag* published the review that was to change the entire course of this story. "At the State Opera: Karajan the Miracle". The author of the article, Edwin von der Nüll, made no bones about his admiration for the thirty-year-old Kapellmeister from Aachen: "This man is the greatest conducting sensation of the century [...] Karajan gave two extraordinary concerts with the Philharmonic. Three weeks ago Karajan surpassed this impression with his debut at the State Opera. What he demonstrated yesterday verges on the inconceivable. A thirty-year-old man pulls off an accomplishment for which our great fifty-year-olds would rightly envy him."

Furtwängler was beside himself. And that even though von der Nüll had already dedicated several poems to him. None of that counted now. The conductor demanded openly that something be done about this "business". His will was done. Von der Nüll kept

his position as critic, but never again reviewed a Furtwängler concert. "Colleague Ka." felt Furtwängler's unleashed wrath as well. After Karajan's third concert at the head of the Berlin Philharmonic on April 14, 1939, one of the performed works, Tchaikovsky's *Pathétique*, was recorded by Polydor. Furtwängler had just produced *Pathétique* for EMI, and when he heard the news, he seethed. He did not (and could not) prevent further recordings, but he could prevent Karajan from appearing at the Philharmonic. Between 1938 and 1942 Karajan managed to conduct only six concerts at the Philharmonic.

It was the same story in Vienna. At the turn of 1938/39 Furtwängler threatened to leave the State Opera if Karajan was invited. And so, as in Berlin, evasive action was taken. At the suggestion of Rudolf Vedder, an influential concert agent of the day, and with Tietjen's blessing, Karajan took on the Sunday concerts of the Berliner Staatskapelle. He also conducted performances at the Opera, such as the world premiere of the opera *The Citizens of Calais* by Rudolf Wagner-Régeny in January 1939.

The next blow came a few months later. On June 2, 1939 a special performance of the *Mastersingers* was held in the State Opera in honor of Prince Paul of Yugoslavia. In the audience, where Göring and Goebbels sat next to the guest of honor, was Adolf Hitler. Hitler, hearing Karajan for the first time, was anything but favorably impressed. He complained about the "bad conducting"; it was not "German" enough. Party membership was of little use here. Under political pressure, Tietjen removed Karajan from the podium for all subsequent *Mastersingers* – so enraging Karajan that he almost lost control of himself. What he did not lose was the memory of the incident: "He [Tietjen] said to me: 'When Furtwängler enters this building, leave by the back door. Don't even try to understand it. That's high politics.'"

Karajan garnered more ovations on February 18, 1940 for his interpretation (from memory) of *Elektra* at the State Opera. After that, however, the climate in Berlin turned chilly. Though not dropped entirely, Karajan fared a bit like Icarus – he had come too close to the sun. But he did not let himself be deterred by this temporary setback. He maintained a cool demeanor, even continuing to faithfully attend Furtwängler's concerts. He sensed that his time would come. Besides, there were the satisfactions of private life. In 1939 Herbert von Karajan met twenty two-year-old Anna Maria Gütermann, scion of the eponymous silk manufacturing dynasty – a charming, charismatic young woman, no fool and pretty besides. On the spot he was carried away by Anita, as her friends called her. He wooed her, even wrote her love letters, finally making her a proposal of marriage, even though his marriage with Elmy was still valid (until

1942). And as always he achieved his desired goal, albeit with unorthodox methods. Just before a performance at the State Opera he called the object of his affections and told her that if she turned down his proposal, he would not begin. She accepted, and he conducted.

As his conducting was increasingly taking place elsewhere than Aachen, Otto Kirchner, who had succeeded Dr. Gross as artistic director, terminated his contract at the end of the 1941/42 season. Karajan, with the Berlin State Opera in Rome at the time, was shocked at the news. The next piece of bad tidings was not long in the offing. In the night of April 9-10, the Berlin State Opera was destroyed by an allied bombing raid. From then on the opera productions were held in the Kroll Opera, while concerts took place in the Old Philharmonic: Furtwängler's sacred hall. Karajan spent these weeks traveling back and forth between Berlin and Aachen, where he produced his own staging of *Der Rosenkavalier* in his last season. For Verdi's *Falstaff* he left the direction to Walter Felsenstein, an important theater figure who would later open the Berlin Comic Opera with a *Fledermaus* in 1946. By then Karajan was no longer in Germany.

### A New Beginning with a Few Catches

On February 18, 1945, right after a concert in the Beethoven Hall, he and his wife had left the capital of the German Reich by plane, heading for Milan. From there, with a stop on Lake Como, they went on to Trieste. An old friend put Karajan up in his villa and arranged for Karajan to give three concerts with the orchestra of the Trieste Theater. Soon thereafter, with the help of the Allies, the couple managed to return to Salzburg, where they stayed in Karajan's parental home. After some initial difficulties, Otto de Pasetti, the top US cultural officer of the Allied commission for the rehabilitation of Austrian cultural workers, helped him to obtain permission to perform, whereupon Franz Sedlak, orchestra chairman of the Vienna Philharmonic, invited him to give concerts in Vienna. Karajan chose his beloved *Don Juan* and Brahms' First. A performance date was fixed, and the rehearsals went well. Then came the setback: the Soviet authorities refused to grant Karajan a permit. Pasetti and Sedlak exerted all their negotiating skills to prevent a cancellation. The concert took place, and Karajan and the Vienna Philharmonic met with an enthusiastic reception. This was promptly followed by a slap in the face. A planned second performance was irrevocably doomed by the Soviets' veto. This time they meant business: soldiers barred the entrance to the concert hall.

### A Visit from London

Karajan waited. And it almost looked as though his patience would pay off. In March 1946 the conductor received permission from the Austrian authorities to conduct in his homeland, albeit with restrictions. Once again, though, the Allies intervened. On June 21 they forbade all public performances until further notice. This did not deter the organizers of the Salzburg Festival, who did not want to give up Karajan at any cost. Though the conductor did not officially appear on the podium at any of the premiers (he was in the prompt box), the entire preparations for the *Rosenkavalier* and *Figaro* lay in his hands. He received other kinds of support as well. At the beginning of the year Vienna was visited by an Englishman who held two influential positions at once: he was the artistic director of the record company EMI and manager of the Philharmonia Orchestra. It was to him, most of all, that Karajan owed the world fame that has reverberated to this day. His name was Walter Legge.

The two met for the first time on January 19, 1946. The atmosphere was one of friendly reserve; after all, it was a matter of business. And they soon got down to business. Three months previously, Walter Legge had founded the Philharmonia Orchestra with the express purpose of making recordings "by whose high standard public performances and future artists will be measured", in the words of Legge's credo. With Karajan, he believed he had found the right man to realize his ambitious project. After brief negotiations, Legge and Karajan came to an agreement. And by September 1946 the conductor entered the studio on Abbey Road to record Beethoven's Eighth Symphony – with the Vienna Philharmonic, however, not the Londoners. It was something of a test run before the real thing. If Karajan was successful with the Vienna Philharmonic, Legge would entrust him unreservedly with his Philharmonia Orchestra.

By the time Karajan embarked on the project, another bothersome affair had finally been cleared up. In October 1947 the conductor's stage ban was finally lifted. At the end of the month Karajan conducted the Vienna Philharmonic in Bruckner's Eighth (without soldiers at the door), and just before Christmas he triumphed with Beethoven's Ninth, which EMI captured on record even before the concert. Then, in 1948, Karajan made his first recording with the Philharmonia Orchestra together with the legendary pianist Dinu Lipatti. To this day even Karajan's critics rave about the elaborate interpretation of the Schumann piano concerto. It was followed by a potpourri. *Don Juan* went without saying, along with Stravinsky's *Jeu de cartes*, symphonies by Beethoven, Brahms, Sibelius, Mozart, Balakirev and Roussel, and Bach's Mass in B Minor. Recording activities centered around several opera productions whose lofty artistic stature has remained unchallenged to this day, culminating in two sublime Mozart interpretations: *Le nozze di Figaro* from 1952 and *Così fan tutte* from the year 1954. These were joined by the Strauss operas

*Der Rosenkavalier* and *Ariadne auf Naxos*, Verdi's *Falstaff* and *Die Fledermaus* by Johann Strauss.

## Jealousy Is Not a Virtue

Karajan's collaboration with Walter Legge worked out beautifully, lasting until 1956. The key advantage was that both were lovers of perfection. His career could have made strides elsewhere as well, but over and over again Furtwängler threw a monkey wrench into the works. In the winter of 1946/47 Karajan attempted a reconciliation with the crusty old man on a hike over the snowy Arlberg Range, but in vain. And he nearly lost his life in the process: returning over the pass he got caught in a snowstorm and had to be rescued by a search party. Furtwängler hurled his thunderbolts like a temperamental weather god.

It was the same story in summer 1948. Karajan conducted the opening premiere of the Salzburg Festival, Gluck's *Orpheus* and *Eurydice*, while Furtwängler conducted *Fidelio*. Walter Legge, who was playing a dangerous game with his plans to produce recordings with both artists, made one last attempt at mediation. Legge invited Karajan and Furtwängler, along with their wives, Eliette and Elisabeth, to dinner in the private dining chamber of the Kasererbräu Hotel. They dined together, conversed and even joked cheerfully. But as soon as the candles were blown out, the feud went on. The very next morning Furtwängler put pressure on a member of the Festival board of trustees, the fickle Egon Hilbert, to bar Karajan from the Festival. Only then, he declared, would he be prepared to sign a contract tying him to Salzburg. Hilbert gave in, and the rest of the Festival management followed suit. *The Magic Flute* which Karajan had claimed for the next year, was taken away from him, with the result that the furious conductor canceled his *Rosenkavalier* as well.

Karajan would not conduct in Salzburg again until the end of 1954. This did not alter his recognition of the other man's charisma, the "major influence" he exerted upon him, an influence "perhaps as strong as that of Toscanini". Furtwängler became a counterpoint for him, an antiphon. Long afterwards in the 1960s Karajan admitted to friends, not without a touch of bitterness, how greatly Furtwängler's attacks had burdened him. Nonetheless, at the critical moment Karajan displayed magnanimity. When Wilhelm Furtwängler was laid to rest in Heidelberg's Bergfriedhof on December 4, 1954, a wreath lay on his grave with the words: "In the loyal spirit of the Berlin Philharmonic – Herbert von Karajan".

In Vienna, too, the jealous Furtwängler exercised a powerful influence. Karajan made do by conducting the Symphony more frequently, instead of the Philharmonic, giving his postwar debut with the Symphony on February 21, 1948. Incidentally, the intensive partnership had astonishing results: the two Viennese orchestras began to approach each other in quality. Two other relationships of trust developed: in early 1949 Karajan acquired a kind of private secretary whom he soon came to trust implicitly: the loyal André von Mattoni. And Antonio Ghiringhelli, the artistic director of the Teatro alla Scala in Milan, proved to be an outspoken admirer. Ghiringhelli asked Karajan to conduct the premieres of two German operas along with follow-up performances. Karajan agreed, and in the 1950/51 season he conducted *Tannhäuser* and *Don Giovanni* at La Scala. Ghiringhelli was so enthused that he entrusted the conductor with two premieres per season until 1954 and even opened up the Italian repertory for him: at La Scala Karajan produced Donizetti's *Lucia di Lammermoor* with Maria Callas in the title role. This was the production that caused a sensation in Vienna in 1956 at the Scala's guest appearance. After the performance the divine Callas bowed before Karajan and kissed his hand.

## Red Roses for the Burning Torch

But his heart long since belonged to another. In St. Tropez in 1951 he had met and fallen in love with the stunning Eliette Mouret. That same year Karajan debuted at the Bayreuth Festival with the *Meistersinger* and a *Ring* Cycle. It would prove to be a tough job. Karajan had a falling-out with his Brünnhilde. In contrast to many singers who have nothing but positive memories of Karajan, Astrid Varnay took a very critical view of the conductor at that time: "Karajan's beat could sometimes be confusing. Although his upbeat and initial downbeat were always clear, so you at least knew where 'one' was, he would then often start to form circles in the air with his eyes closed. He was enjoying and celebrating the music, sometimes very much for himself."

The very next year in Bayreuth, in the new staging of *Tristan and Isolde* with Ramón Vinay and Astrid Varnay in the title roles, the two disparate natures collided for the second time. Once again "la torche brûlante" ("the burning torch"), as her colleague Régine Crespin once called her, was irritated: "While Vinay and I sat upstage trying to decipher the tempo, Karajan was again down in the pit with his eyes partially closed, sketching clouds in the air with no clear rhythmic structure for us to follow. In an attempt to keep together, at least with one another, Vinay and I simply held hands, and whoever wasn't singing would beat time gently with the thumb on the back of the partner's hand." Upon her return to New York, the singer wrote to the Bayreuth Festival asking not to be considered for future productions conducted by Karajan – an unnecessary action; due to differences of opinion between Karajan and the festival directors, after *Tristan* the Bayreuth chapter was closed for the conductor.

The "burning torch" chapter, however, was not. After twelve years of silence a reunion took place at the Salzburg Festival. Karajan wanted Astrid Varnay to sing the title role in his new production of Strauss's *Elektra*. The contact was established by – who else – the indefatigable mediator Walter Legge. Varnay hesitated, then accepted. The premiere on August 11, 1964, with Karajan at the head of the Vienna Philharmonic, turned out to be a triumph of legendary proportions. On the day of the dress rehearsal "Elektra" found an enormous bouquet of red roses in her dressing room. Attached was an envelope with a short letter from Karajan thanking her for her cooperation in the rehearsals and inviting the singer to a revival in the following year.

## With a Thousand Joys

Was Eliette's influence to thank for such polite, gentlemanly behavior on Karajan's part? Possibly. The fact of the matter is that Karajan blossomed at her side. Photos of the two together show Karajan relaxed, almost cheery. Not that this made him forget to advance his career. His stated aim was now Berlin. To kick off the Festival Weeks in 1953, Karajan conducted the Berlin Philharmonic with the *Eroica* and the Concerto for Orchestra. A clever choice; just previously he had recorded Bartók's complex work with the Philharmonia Orchestra. Critics praised the "combination of ultra-lucid, all-controlling deliberation and magical spontaneity from which the mysterious, dream-like vividness of the musical form emerges."

The following year Karajan returned to the Berlin podium with works by Mozart, Brahms and, once again, Bartók on the program. What the newspapers wrote the next day sounds matter-of-fact, but touches at the heart of the matter: "Karajan has not gone down the path of the wunderkind that so often comes to nothing. He has developed quite naturally into a major, internationally popular conductor," who now had nearly achieved his goal. Furtwängler was approaching death in a sanatorium far from Berlin. And only one serious rival stood in Karajan's way – Sergiu Celibidache.

A professional director could not have stage-managed the following events more suspensefully. In the space of a few days both candidates conducted the orchestra in the hall of the Academy of Music on Hardenbergstraße. Karajan opened in two concerts on November 21 and 22 with the Tallis Fantasia by Ralph Vaughan Williams and an imposing interpretation of Bruckner's Ninth Symphony. Sergiu Celibidache followed in three concerts on November

25, 26 and 29 with a powerful Brahms Requiem and works by Ravel, Bartók and Tiessen. A day later, Furtwängler died. Karajan, now in Rome, received a telegram from Vienna with the words "The king is dead, long live the king!" The next morning artistic director Gerhart von Westerman offered him the vacant post. And by December 13 the orchestra board and the Philharmonic's council of five had already issued a unanimous resolution appointing Karajan chief conductor. The official approval of the Berlin municipal authorities was still outstanding (it was given on April 5, 1955), and another year was to pass before the heir apparent signed the contract (on April 25, 1956), but one thing was clear beyond question: for Herbert von Karajan the dream of a lifetime had come true. He had reached the summit. The official enthronement took place in February 1955. After an enthusiastically received concert with the Berlin Philharmonic, culture senator Tiburtius posed the famous question in front of a circle of German and international journalists: "Would you, Herr von Karajan, be prepared to become Furtwängler's successor?" The still more famous answer was: "Herr Senator, with a thousand joys, I have no other words for it!"

It was an emotional moment. But there was little time for celebration. The Philharmonic was in the midst of planning its six-week North America tour in late February, meant as a gesture of thanks from Berlin for the 1948 Air Bridge. It was the orchestra's first visit to the continent. Suddenly a problem arose. The Berlin-born American manufacturer Henry Reichold had promised to cover the costs of the concert tour, but backed out after Furtwängler's death. Given the great political significance of the tour, the Foreign Office in Bonn, several departments of the Berlin Senate and the Berlin Lottery jumped into the breach. Milan's La Scala, where Karajan was actually supposed to start rehearsing the new production of *The Valkyrie*, also took an accommodating stance. Its intendent in chief Ghiringhelli released the conductor for the duration of the tour.

## The American Dream

The suspense continued. It was no secret in Berlin that the American musicians' union had threatened to strike and that protests were planned – in particular against former Nazi party member Karajan. The officials did their best to come to grips with the situation, and Karajan tried to be appeasing: "We are going to America to bring music and beauty. We want only good, we want no hatred."

Late in the evening of February 106 members of the Philharmonic Orchestra took off from Tempelhof Airport in two Pan American Super Six Clipper planes to start on their tour of the USA and Canada. The new conductor would lead his orchestra a total of twenty-six times. After positively received performances in Washington and Philadelphia, the concert in New York on March 1 turned out to be an acid test. Members of Jewish organizations demonstrated in front of Carnegie Hall and demanded a boycott of the "Nazi" conductor. Inside it was not only warmer and quieter, the atmosphere was more pleasant as well. The Philharmonic played first the American, then the German national anthem before enchanting the audience with works by Haydn, Beethoven and Wagner. The final applause was tumultuous. And as an encore they played the Tannhäuser Overture. Once again, the political will seemed to have bowed before the power of music – the result being that the Philharmonic and Karajan were received far more warmly on their second tour in the fall of 1956.

It had been the same story the previous June. For the first time after being named conductor "for life", Karajan gave a guest appearance with the Berlin Philharmonic at the Mozart Festival in the Viennese capital. Of course the Viennese were listening with bated breath. After Mozart's Haffner Symphony, the prelude and Liebestod from *Tristan und Isolde* and Beethoven's *Eroica*, they felt flattered. And Karajan acquired one of his many titles: he was dubbed "Sun King". This epithet would be remembered for a long time in Vienna.

In the meantime Karajan swept from one triumph to the next. At the beginning of April 1957 he debuted as Artistic Director of the Vienna State Opera with *The Valkyrie*. A fortnight later the curtain went up on a new production of Verdi's *Otello*. Things continued at the same pace. At the Vienna Festival in June Karajan conducted a splendid *Carmen* and a (less splendid) *Traviata*. He had invited his Berlin Philharmonic to their first appearance at the Salzburg Festival that summer. Within the space of two weeks, Karajan was joined at the head of the orchestra by George Szell, Rafael Kubelik and Wolfgang Sawallisch, conductors he much admired. In November the Berlin Philharmonic's first Japanese tour followed, with sixteen concerts in eight cities – a marathon of a program.

## Europe's Generalmusikdirektor

In April 1958 Herbert von Karajan, the Sun King, celebrated his fiftieth birthday. He was unrivaled as the epitome of an interpreter who not only embodied but demonstrated the symbiosis between artistic and economic status in the age of music's technical reproducibility. No one else marketed classical music with as much mass appeal, no one was as effective. His plenitude of power was immense. Karajan was the Artistic Director of the Vienna State Opera. He was the Chief Conductor of the Berlin Philharmonic: for life. He was the favorite guest conductor of La Scala in Milan. He was conductor for a series of subscription concerts of the Vienna Philharmonic.

He was the Concert Director of the Vienna Symphony: for life. He was the absolute ruler of the Salzburg Festival. He was an influential conductor at the Lucerne and Edinburgh Festivals. In this period a joke emerged, circulating in Berlin and later becoming legend. Asked by a taxi driver for his destination, Karajan responded: "Wherever you want, I'm needed everywhere."

Which was no exaggeration. Karajan concerts had cult character. Harold Schonberg was surely close to the truth when he said that, like Bernstein, Karajan embodied "the jet age, the new ideas that were entering music, the new economic and social forces that were having their effect." The music journalist's adjectives for Bernstein and Karajan also reflect the reality: "wealthy, influential, free, ruthless, good-looking, gifted, exerting a magnetic attraction". Schonberg concedes, though, that his success was not due to external factors alone: "Like all outstanding conductors, Karajan possessed that inner rhythm, one both subtle and controlled." And: "He radiates an aura of willpower and authority that subjugates the audience, and even those who do not like his way of making music constantly visit his concerts." Here, in this almost paradoxical charisma, lies Karajan's singularity.

In October 1958 Herbert von Karajan married for the third time. In the French winter sports resort of Mégève he led Eliette Mouret to the altar at last. Soon after their wedding Karajan enjoyed the delights of late fatherhood: Eliette bore him two daughters. At the time of Isabel's birth he was fifty-two; at Arabel's birth he was fifty-six. A man in the best years of his life, as the saying goes. And one who was indeed prone to sentimental gestures. When Karajan bought a two-million-mark yacht to ply the waters of the Mediterranean in style, he gave it the name Helisara VI – a play on the names HErbert, ELIettte, ISAbel and ARAbel.

Before marrying in Mégève he had realized his latest major projects at the Festival in Salzburg, beginning with Verdi's *Don Carlo* directed by Gustav Gründgens. This was followed by the European premiere of the opera *Vanessa* by Samuel Barber. Karajan's engagement with 20th century music was not limited to Barber's stage work. In September 1959, for instance, he conducted the German premiere of Rolf Liebermann's *Capriccio* and Messiaen's *Réveil des oiseaux*.

An important date for him and the Berlin Philharmonic was the 1st of October. On this day Wolfgang Stresemann officially took up his post as artistic director of the orchestra – a stroke of luck for all involved. Even Karajan, who had not exactly favored Stresemann for the position, was increasingly won over by his noblesse and communication talents. Seldom was an artistic director so loyal to his chief conductor. And one thing is certain: the Sun King did not make things easy for Stresemann. As it turned out, Stresemann was helped by the fact that his mother was friends with Karajan's closest collaborator, André von Mattoni, who gave him helpful hints on dealing with the maestro. For instance, Mattoni advised Stresemann always to be present at Berlin's Tegel Airport to greet Karajan when he arrived. Sure enough, Karajan was delighted, and decided to combine business with pleasure: in the coming years, many of the Berlin Philharmonic's programs were worked out during the ride between the airport and the hotel. No friendship developed; over the decades the conductor and the artistic director maintained a polite yet distant relationship. Once, however, there was a moment of intimacy. Stresemann managed to convince Culture Senator Tiburtius to raise Karajan's pay from two to three thousand marks. After learning this at dinner at the Ritz, Karajan put his arm around Stresemann's shoulders.

### A Hall for Salzburg

On July 25, 1960 Herbert von Karajan fulfilled a dream. Salzburg celebrated the opening of the new Festival Hall, designed by the architect Clemens Holzmeister. The scale verged on the Olympian, with a price tag to match: the building sucked up a total of 210 million schillings. With an area of 1600 square meters and a maximum of 30 meters in breadth, the stage surpassed all precedents. The 2164 seats seemed almost modest in comparison. The temple to the muses was opened with Mozart's Coronation Mass and the Gloria from his Mass in C Minor. Karajan conducted. And of course he was also at the podium for the first opera premiere in the Festival Hall, Strauss's *Rosenkavalier*. Years later the participants recalled the enchanting performance. In the meantime some changes had taken place in the Festival administration. The new boss was Bernhard Paumgartner. He did not see eye to eye with his former pupil, and a month after the opening Karajan stepped down from the Festival's board of directors. It took four years for the two pugnacious men to come to an agreement – favorable for Karajan – on who was the master of the new hall.

August 13, 1961 changed the face of the world. The Berlin Wall went up. The shock went deep. Nonetheless, the Berlin Philharmonic set out on its third North American tour. The program was truly Herculean: twenty-four concerts in five weeks. The orchestra and its conductor were celebrated deliriously. The relationship grew and flourished, culminating at year's end in the first of a total of three complete recordings of the Beethoven symphonies. During this period Karajan was already busy with the preparations for his next

new production at the Vienna State Opera. For Claude Debussy's hundredth birthday Karajan presented his opera *Pelléas et Mélisande*. It was the beginning of a long collaboration with set designer Günther Schneider-Siemssen, who would design the sets for nearly all of Karajan's productions from then on. Even during the rehearsals conflicts arose. The stage workers went on strike. The Viennese bureaucracy dug in its heels. Karajan resigned from his position as artistic director – only to resign from his resignation a few weeks later.

### The (Temporary) End of an Era

In Berlin things were working out better, no doubt largely because Karajan was better able to enforce his will. The hall of the Berlin Philharmonic opened on October 15, 1963. As always when something revolutionary was in the works, Karajan played a crucial role in its success. Just before the decision was to be made, Hans Scharoun's brilliant design came in for criticism, and a much more conventional proposal threatened to win the competition. Karajan intervened forcefully: "Gentlemen, it goes without saying that only Scharoun's architecture comes in question."

For the opening, he conducted his Berlin Philharmonic in Beethoven's Ninth. The harmony between the orchestra and its conductor had reached its first zenith. This was acknowledged even in Vienna when Karajan gave a guest performance there in May 1964 with a Brahms program. The concert was a revelation. But it intensified a conflict that seemed inevitable. Karajan's exclusive contract with Deutsche Grammophon tied Karajan to the Berlin Philharmonic, and of course he recorded the Beethoven symphonies with this orchestra. There was a storm of angry protest from the Vienna Philharmonic. Karajan retorted coolly: "It's my affair who I record my records with." On another occasion, when asked by a reporter which of the two orchestras was dearer to him, he responded with a delicacy worthy of Solomon that he felt like a Mohammedan with his two favorite wives – his heart was big enough for both.

Vienna held its breath. In June 1964, after an eight-year reign, Herbert von Karajan resigned as Artistic Director of the State Opera. In so doing he left the scene of his greatest triumphs to date, and of the most vehement hostility. Karajan's disciples and critics were pitted against one another. His supporters cited the many splendid evenings which had made Vienna a place of pilgrimage for music lovers from around the world, who came in part for Karajan and the Vienna Philharmonic, but also to hear the world-class singers who performed there: Maria Callas, Leontyne Price, Renata Tebaldi, Mirella Freni, Giuseppe di Stefano, Mario del Monaco, Franco Corelli. His detractors countered with Karajan's extravagance: just the wigs for *Tannhäuser* had cost a trifling 100,000 schillings. An additional argument for those who dearly wanted to give Karajan the boot was that he had supposedly favored Italian singers to an inappropriate extent (Karajan made an ironic joke of the accusation at a press conference when he told an Italian journalist that he could not offer her a Cinzano, otherwise he would immediately be accused of Italianization). And the boss had fulfilled his duties far too rarely, came the indignant cry from his enemies' camp.

### It Can't Be Played Better

Karajan sulked. But Vienna was not the world. The fourth North America tour with the Berlin Philharmonic in early 1965 turned out to be a triumph; Karajan's Beethoven interpretations met with frenetic praise. Noteworthy are the words of the critic Louis Biancolli: "It is clear to me that this man is a genius. Nine-tenths titanic, one tenth indefinable epiphany." In May the "genius" took his orchestra to Scandinavia. For Jean Sibelius's hundredth birthday they performed his Fourth and Fifth Symphonies in Helsinki, renderings that have etched themselves into the memories of all present. When artistic director Stresemann went to Karajan to thank him after the concerts, all Karajan replied was: "It can't be played any better than that." That evening Karajan had another surprise up his sleeve. He, who despised dinners and parties from the depths of his soul, appeared at the reception and spoke unprompted of Sibelius, of his admiration for the composer. The previous day he had visited Sibelius's house in Järvenpää and laid down a wreath on his grave. Karajan, the sphinx.

Further tours took him and the Berlin Philharmonic to Lucerne, Venice, Athens, Milan and Epidaurus. There, in a Greek theater from the fourth century B. C., Karajan conducted Verdi's *Requiem*. In January 1967 the same work was to seal an artistic liaison between two great individualists. Karajan met the nouvelle-vague director Henri-Georges Clouzot, whose film *The Wages of Fear* had achieved cult status, and together they produced five films for television under the title *The Art of Conducting*. The collaboration ended with the film on Verdi's *Requiem* in La Scala in Milan; the aesthetic concepts were too disparate. However, Karajan's fascination with the artistic genre continued unabated, documented by a number of home videos he produced himself from then on.

### A Wonderful Easter Egg

When Karajan assumed the directorship of the Vienna State Opera in 1957, he chose a beloved work from his childhood, Wagner's *The Valkyrie*. Now, ten years later, he turned to this opera once again. This time, too, the occasion was a special one: the founding of the Salzburg Easter Festival. In a letter to Maria Callas, Walter Legge called it "a wonderful Easter egg". And Karajan, too, reacted with unbridled enthusiasm: "They'll come at Easter. Experts, devotees, and of course people with money too. The best audience in the world is here, here is the quintessence of the German intellectual elite."

The undertaking had been prepared long in advance, and despite costs of 1.5 million marks for artists' and technicians' fees, the financial risk was low. As a safety net, Karajan had launched an association of friends and supporters. The system was a clever one. Due to the anticipated publicity, many affluent fans were all too willing to join the association as patrons. And thus Artistic Director, Manager, Conductor and Stage Director Karajan exulted after the end of the first festival with a visible touch of self-irony: "I won't have to go to debtors' prison. Of course, I can't pay myself. In materialistic terms, I go away empty-handed. But artistically I'm 100 percent fulfilled."

Of course, the maestro was not telling the whole truth here. Before *The Valkyrie* went onstage in Salzburg, Karajan had produced the work with the Berlin Philharmonic in Berlin. His salary was 100,000 marks. So much for the debtors' prison. But it was about more than money, it was about fame, about prestige. All that was a means to an end for Karajan, and the end was the mastery of the art, by him. "What was important for me", said Karajan, "was the human situation of the Ring – which of course is told through the story of the gods: when is one free, when is one unfree? After all, everything can be bought…" Here he unintentionally reveals the supreme principle of his life: the search for freedom that is an addiction to freedom. In this connection it is illuminating to look at an appraisal given in July 1968 by the Viennese graphologist Claire Knoll when presented with the handwriting of the unidentified Karajan: "An uncommonly gifted individualist whose plans, expectations and exaggerated emotions are fascinating because he heroizes his imaginative life, feels and judges enthusiastically, and despite his censoriousness and his remarkable vitality always remains in some way an outsider who, if he overestimates himself, can be a strain on the world around him. He makes and lives his own heaven." Was there ever a more penetrating analysis of Karajan?

### Onward to Moscow!

In October 1967 Karajan flew across the Atlantic once again. In Montreal he conducted *La Bohème*, in New York Verdi's Requiem, both with the orchestra of the Teatro alla Scala. Plans for a more intensive collaboration between him and the Chicago Symphony Orchestra were developed and abandoned. Another partnership was doomed from the outset. On November 6, 1968, Charles Munch, chief conductor of the Orchestre de Paris, died. French president Georges Pompidou personally asked Karajan for help. Karajan agreed to take on the orchestra as Conseiller musical, though he was severely overstretched by concerts and recordings with the Berlin and Vienna Philharmonics and the planning of the Easter Festival. The inevitable happened: in May 1970, when Culture Minister Edmond Michelet urged him to attend more closely to the Parisian ensemble, Karajan resigned from his position.

In the meantime he had become an honorary citizen of Berlin, a privilege awarded on his sixtieth birthday – amusingly enough, considering that Karajan never settled down on the Spree. After a number of years in the venerable Hotel Savoy, he always spent his Berlin sojourns in a suite at the Kempinski. Now that he was being hustled from one honor to the next, there was still just one thing he wanted: to flee from the chattering crowds and into the auditorium, into the arms of art. Even during the festivities for his sixtieth birthday he did not cancel the two rehearsals that were scheduled.

Parallel to this, preparations for a very special project for the promotion of young talent were underway. On September 25 Karajan signed the charter of the foundation that would bear his name. For him it was about more than just his name, though, as became clear in 1977 when he received the Ernst von Siemens Music Prize. The prize money, totaling 100,000 Swiss francs, went directly into the foundation's coffers. One year later he initiated the Herbert von Karajan Competition for conductors in Berlin.

He had already been there with the Scala, with the Vienna Philharmonic too. Now, in the fall of 1968, he wanted to present his family in the Soviet Union at last. And as everyone knows: when Herbert von Karajan decided to do something, he got his way. It was true in this case as well. Once the highest political bodies had come to an agreement, the Berlin Philharmonic, with Karajan at its head, headed east at the end of May. To avoid flying from Schönefeld Airport in East Berlin, Karajan and the orchestra first traveled to Prague, where they gave a jubilantly received concert, and then on to Moscow. The reception was cool. Before the first of the three planned concerts the Philharmonic was announced as "a symphony orchestra from West Berlin". Karajan fumed, threatening to depart immediately unless an announcement was made before the second concert correcting the error. Evidently even the Soviets were impressed by this attitude; the mistake was corrected. The concert had barely begun when an incident occurred: during the first bars of Beethoven's *Pastorale* a door was flung open and a handful of young enthusiasts stormed the hall. To avoid creating a scene, they were allowed to have their way. It was not to be the only curious incident on the tour. A planned recep-

tion on the day between the concerts in Moscow and Leningrad (the latter in the presence of Dmitri Shostakovich, with a moving rendition of his Tenth) was canceled by the Soviets on the grounds that the orchestra would have to depart earlier due to fog in Leningrad. The sun had been shining there for days. Karajan responded to the latest affront with British humor. Asked to leave the plane after landing in Leningrad, he ostentatiously remained seated, claiming to be afraid of the fog.

## Unplanned Pit Stops and Orchestra Pits

At this time Berlin and its Philharmonic were Karajan's artistic home. This also played a crucial role when negotiating contracts with the two leading classical music labels. In the fall of 1970 Karajan signed two similar contracts with EMI and with Deutsche Grammophon. Both contracts guaranteed him at least ten recordings per year and the freedom to sell Decca any recordings which neither of the two labels wanted. Karajan received royalties of ten percent. Audiences around the world profited from this deal as well. In 1970 the *Ring* was completed and released on Deutsche Grammophon, and EMI brought out a *Fidelio* recording.

Beethoven's opera, which Karajan had put on the agenda of the Easter Festival for 1971, one year late to celebrate the birthday of the composer (born in 1770), very nearly became his last recording. On the morning of the premiere Karajan spontaneously decided to try out a new racing car. Near Salzburg the car hit a rough spot, skidded and turned over – making a pit stop in the roadside ditch. With difficulty, Karajan clambered out of the wreck, suffering from shock, but uninjured – and stood in the orchestra pit that very evening.

Was it obsession? The craving for validation? The will to omnipotence? Probably it was a combination of all of them that drove Karajan – drove him further and further. In Berlin in 1972 he realized his third pioneering project for the promotion of young talent – the Orchestra Academy of the Berlin Philharmonic – with the financial assistance of the head of the Dresdner Bank, Jürgen Ponto. No sooner was that done when he got the idea of initiating the Salzburg Whitsun Festival in honor of Anton Bruckner. When the news spread that he wanted to commit his Berlin Philharmonic as the regular orchestra, he was subjected to increasingly vocal criticism in Berlin, as people complained about the frequent absences of the orchestra and its conductor. Karajan, Stresemann and the city's cultural senator held a discussion to clarify the matter, and in the end all the parties went home satisfied. The senator, because Berlin would get a mini-festival of its own starting at the turn of 1973/74. Karajan, because he was able to keep his Whitsun Festival. And the artistic director, because his mediation had been successful.

## The Sickness Almost Unto Death

In the fall of 1975 Karajan made a guest appearance with the Berlin Philharmonic in Teheran for the dedication of an underground concert hall. Eliette and their two daughters accompanied him. Two performances were open to the public. The third, a private event in honor of the controversial potentate, presented difficulties. According to the custom of the country, the concert had to begin the moment the Shah took his seat. Karajan had to be persuaded to bow to this unaccustomed hierarchy. He gave in reluctantly.

Back in Berlin, at the beginning of December Karajan conducted Bruckner's monumental Eighth two times in the space of sixteen hours. He was suffering from unbearable back pain. Afterwards he traveled to St. Moritz to spend the Christmas holidays there with his family. The pain refused to subside, and a doctor Karajan consulted advised an immediate operation. The advice saved his life. A slipped disk was pressing into the spinal cord, threatening Karajan with paraplegia. In Zurich the specialist Dr. Majdid Samii operated on him for five hours.

Seven years later Samii and Karajan met again under similarly unpleasant circumstances. Once again the spinal cord was pinched; once again the doctor saved the artists' mobility, but discovered significant signs of weakness and paralysis in the muscles of his upper and lower limbs.

In 1978 Karajan had already suffered a stroke during rehearsal – which did not prevent his rapid return to the podium. The same was true in 1976. On March 3 he stood in front of his orchestra again as if nothing had happened – a superhuman effort, but characteristic of his formidable will. At the Easter Festival Karajan subsequently conducted *Lohengrin* (in his own staging) and a wonderful Verdi Requiem.

## Red Carpet Treatment

At next year's Salzburg Festival Karajan produced Strauss's *Salome*. His innocently corrupt heroine was Hildegard Behrens. He had discovered her, and now he made her great. Her story illustrates how intuitively Karajan made the right moves when searching for the ideal singer for a given role. In Düsseldorf for a concert, he learned that the dress rehearsal for Alban Berg's *Wozzeck* was being held in the opera house and was urged to go listen to the singer performing Marie. Karajan went, and a few seconds later he knew: That's her, that's my *Salome*, I've waited twenty-eight years for

this moment. He engaged the young artist on the spot. After several months' preparation he recorded *Salome* with her and then invited her to Salzburg.

Hildegard Behrens was not the only singer who owed her international career to Karajan. Gundula Janowitz, Leontyne Price, Agnes Baltsa, Helga Dernesch, Anna Tomova-Sintow and Katia Ricciarelli – all were his discoveries. José Carreras, José van Dam and Jon Vickers also profited from Karajan's appreciation and loyalty. Christa Ludwig, who called him "le bon Dieu" said: "Karajan gave singers the red carpet treatment: he created a tapestry of sound, and one only had to lay one's voice upon it."

Karajan's nurturing approach can also be seen in the case of the violinist Anne-Sophie Mutter. After auditioning for him in 1976, the thirteen-year-old was first engaged for Mozart's Third Violin Concerto at the Salzburg Whitsun Festival. She played the same piece a year later in Berlin. Not until 1980 did Karajan produce the Beethoven concerto with her.

## Return of the Prodigal Son

May 8, 1977, was a Sunday, Mother's Day. The sky over Vienna was cloudless. On that day the State Opera, the Austrian capital's sacred temple to the muses, was transformed into a madhouse. It was a miracle that no one fainted. From the galleries chants of "Ka-ra-jan, Ka-ra-jan!" resounded through the hall. Boundless rejoicing for a man who never wanted to conduct here again. For thirteen years the city had been under the master's spell. Since fall 1976 the way was clear again. Karajan's old friend Egon Seefehlner, director of the State Opera, presented Karajan with a contract that elevated him de facto and de jure to absolute ruler of the house. Karajan signed on April 13. The most important passage in the contract stated that from 1978 he would be permitted "to make the artistic products available to broad segments of the population using the most modern instruments of the mass media". In addition, he received an additional 21,000 mark rehearsal fee per evening, which automatically incurred the envy of those who accused him of absolutism. But those who pitched their tents at night in front of the Opera to get their hands on one of the 2200 tickets were moved in a very different way by the return of the prodigal son. Karajan was a magnet. Thirty thousand requests for tickets were received for his concert of Beethoven symphonies. Herbert von Karajan conducted nine concerts in May 1977 at the Vienna State Opera, three performances apiece of *Il Trovatore*, *Figaro* and *Bohème*. All of them were sold out far in advance. After the final performance of Puccini's Bohemian opera, the ovations lasted for three quarters of an hour.

But more honors were to come for the "slender Caesar" (stern). For his seventieth birthday Karajan received the gold Hans von Bülow medal from the hands of the Berlin Philharmonic. The following January he celebrated his fiftieth year as a conductor. The Berlin Philharmonic had not forgotten the occasion. At the start of a concert on January 27, 1979, they paid their respects to their boss with a flourish and an intrada.

### The Screen Remains Black

"The sound of silence" would be a good heading for the TV dispute that ruffled feathers that same year. Its background was an absurd disparity: while Germany's ARD channel was capable of broadcasting every performance in stereo, the ZDF channel lacked these technical capabilities. Karajan, contractually obliged to provide the ZDF with four concerts annually – eagerly anticipated by an audience of millions – now demanded acoustic justice. To put enough pressure behind his demand, he made an ultimatum. Either the ZDF would be given the same stereo capabilities as its competitor, the ARD, or he would refuse to appear on German television with the Berlin Philharmonic ever again. The rub of the matter was that meanwhile the ARD had bought recordings of the nine Beethoven symphonies – not with Karajan and his Berliners, but with Bernstein and the Vienna Philharmonic. No sooner had the smoke cleared, than the next conflict came knocking. There were plans for Eurovision to broadcast the premiere of *Don Carlo* in the Vienna State Opera on May 9, 1980, in fourteen countries, but this was thwarted by a veto from Karajan, who was acting both as director and conductor. The reason was a dispute about the rights. Three of the singers taking part in Karajan's Salzburg staging of the Verdi opera were bound by contract to media entrepreneur Leo Kirch's film and television production company Unitel for the planned filming. Karajan justified his veto on the grounds that the exclusive contract between the artists and the TV production company had been terminated too late. The Austrian television company (Österreichisches Fernsehen, ORF) responded that all the conditions demanded by Karajan had been fulfilled. What followed was the game of intrigues and backstabbing typical of such cases of twisted reality. There was a barrage of abuse, denials and legal hairsplitting. In the end, the screen remained black.

### In a Clinch over a Clarinet

At about this time, by the grace of Karajan as it were, the discussion of who should succeed him at the head of the Berlin Philharmonic Orchestra and the Berliner Philharmonic began. There was much whispering, and the phalanx of those deemed worthy to tread in the titan's footsteps included many prominent names. Lorin Maazel and Seiji Ozawa were named, along with Zubin Mehta, Daniel Barenboim, Klaus Tennstädt, James Levine, Riccardo Muti and Claudio Abbado. Karajan did not find it at all irreverent to conduct the discussion in public; he named Mehta, Ozawa and Tennstädt as his favorites. He set one condition. "Whoever it is, he must not be the chief conductor of another orchestra. In my day I gave up practically everything to become chief conductor for life. That proved to be the right decision, and my successor must abide by it as well."

Truth is an elastic concept. Europe's Generalmusikdirektor was indeed a Jack of all trades; he occupied central positions and thus had a great deal of power. But it must be kept in mind that all his life Karajan refused to work as a guest conductor with orchestras other than his Berliners and the Vienna Philharmonic. He stood by this decision – with one exception. In Salzburg and Lucerne he conducted the Cleveland Orchestra at the request of its conductor, George Szell. The experience had quite an effect – afterwards he rehearsed the Berlin Philharmonic with such unaccustomed intensity that its concerned artistic director, Wolfgang Stresemann, asked him the reason for the work mania. Karajan replied with captivating conciseness: "After my experience with the Cleveland Orchestra I wanted to prove to myself that I have the best orchestra in the world after all."

In 1982 the best orchestra in the world had every reason to celebrate. The Berlin Philharmonic turned one hundred years young. Despite a lingering case of the flu, Karajan conducted the jubilee concerts on March 30 and April 1 with Mozart's Jupiter Symphony, the Eroica and Mahler's Ninth. With an effort, he saw through the anniversary visit to Vienna. After that he collapsed; malaria was suspected. But the phoenix rose again. Just one month later, in Hamburg, Karajan presented the world's first industrially produced compact disc. It captured Strauss's symphonic poem *An Alpine Symphony*, interpreted by the Berlin Philharmonic with Herbert von Karajan. It was the dawn of a new age on the record market. In the years to come he recorded all of Beethoven's symphonies with his orchestra for a third time. Though the interpretation did not measure up to the previous recordings, the digital recording technology guaranteed – as it had before in the *Parsifal* recording – the best possible quality. Karajan called it a "tool for the musicians to work more precisely, better, with fewer disruptive noises."

There were disruptive noises of a very different kind when a young clarinetist from the Bavarian Radio Symphony Orchestra won the audition for the vacant soloist position. Karajan wanted her, even if the Devil himself were to stand in his way, and the orchestra did not want her. A three-year-long squabble developed. In the end, Sabine Meyer voluntarily forewent the position. The affair permanently damaged the trust between the conductor and the orchestra. And when the conflict began, Wolfgang Stresemann was no longer in office. The new artistic director was Peter Girth, who had nothing remotely approaching his predecessor's sensitivity. This led to additional fallings-out, threats, cancellations, in short: to all kinds of childishness. And finally, at Whitsun 1984, to a rupture between Karajan and the Berlin Philharmonic. The conductor uninvited his orchestra from the Festival – and invited the Vienna Philharmonic instead. At that the Berliners indirectly demanded Karajan's resignation. Fortunately, in the midst of this hopeless muddle (artistic director Girth had been sent on a "long vacation"), Wolfgang Stresemann entered the stage again. And lo and behold, the impossible came to pass. After a tenacious tug of war, the famous Berlin peace treaty was concluded. At the Festival Karajan conducted the Berlin Philharmonic in Bach's Mass in B Minor. With peace just barely restored, they headed for Japan. Eliette von Karajan accompanied her husband, with good reason: the year before he had had to undergo a second difficult intervertebral disk operation. This did not prevent him, though, from resuming his helicopter flying lessons a few weeks later and conducting his sixth *Rosenkavalier* at the Salzburg Festival.

### A Child and an Old Chinese Wise Man

All the same, Karajan sensed that his strength was waning. At the 1985 Salzburg Festival he conducted for the first time from a seated position. That same year the readers of the French magazine *Diapason* voted him the most popular contemporary classical musician, ahead of even Montserrat Caballé and Mstislav Rostropovich. Karajan fulfilled yet another dream: at a High Mass celebrated by Pope John Paul II at St. Peter's, he conducted Mozart's Coronation Mass, the same work he had chosen once before at the opening of the Salzburg Festival Hall. His partners were the Vienna Philharmonic and the Wiener Singverein. Kathleen Battle sang an unforgettable Agnus Dei. And Herbert von Karajan, visibly moved, received communion from the hands of the Pope himself.

The time of partings was approaching, beginning with Wolfgang Stresemann. In February 1986 he stepped down for the second time, this time for good. Karajan, now equally resembling a child and an old Chinese wise man, increasingly sought out works with a premonition of death. At the Easter Festival he juxtaposed Verdi's *Don Carlo* with Bruckner's Ninth Symphony. In May he recorded Mozart's Requiem for film and CD with the Vienna Philharmonic. It was one of his most impressive recordings. At the 1987 Festival he conducted a new production of *Don Giovanni*, and in the summer he invited Jessye Norman to Salzburg to conduct – for the last time

– several pieces by Wagner: the "Tannhäuser Overture", the "Siegfried Idyll" and the prelude and "Liebestod" from *Tristan*. At such moments Karajan felt that the end was approaching. But this did not prevent him from opening the Chamber Music Hall of the Berlin Philharmonic in October 1987 with a fanfare by Boris Blacher composed especially for the occasion and then, from the harpsichord, leading the Philharmonic strings and Anne-Sophie Mutter in Vivaldi's Four Seasons.

The next year's Salzburg Easter Festival proved disappointing. In particular, the new production of *Tosca* was poorly received. The day after the end of the Festival Karajan celebrated his eightieth birthday. EMI re-released a large portion of the archive. Deutsche Grammophon retaliated with a special edition of twenty five silver discs, their covers adorned with Eliette's landscape paintings. Two more biographies appeared, a film, countless articles. Little of it was to Karajan's taste. He accepted only the book by Franz Endler, because it gave him the chance to have his say.

A touch of bitterness was unmistakable. Karajan admitted: "The greatest burden for me is that my illness bars me from nearly all kinds of sports. I was very active all my life, and now I know that especially in sports I put in so much that the physical consequences are now doubly severe. It is a great blow to me that I can no longer ski, that I've had to give up my yacht, that mountain hikes are now out of the question. And another critical change in my life is that I can no longer take the hour-long walks I used to take at all hours of the day and night." According to Karajan, "Of all these things, all I am left with is my daily swim. The many operations and the infections I have had several times recently have forced me to stay at home. I sit and study my scores and work on my films. I see that as a caesura that has been decreed in my life, and I see that I am forced to find the meaning in it."

At the end of August 1988 Karajan stepped down from the board of directors of the Salzburg Festival. Shortly after that a special encounter took place. Karajan met Bernstein, who had conducted the Berlin Philharmonic in Mahler's Ninth on October 4 as part of the Berlin Festival Weeks, a benefit concert for Amnesty International. On New Year's Eve, 1988, Karajan conducted his last concert in Berlin. In a subtle irony of fate, at his side sat a wunderkind such as he himself might once have been. Yevgeny Kissin played Tchaikovsky's Piano Concerto in B Minor. That February Herbert von Karajan celebrated one last great triumph, flying to New York for three concerts with the Vienna Philharmonic. At Carnegie Hall he conducted Schubert's Unfinished Symphony twice; the third concert was of Bruckner's Eighth. The silence after the conclusion was almost uncanny.

What followed was almost uncanny as well. On April 23, after an unsatisfactory Easter Festival, Herbert von Karajan conducted in public for the last time. At a Sunday matinee the Sunday's child conducted a performance of Bruckner's Seventh Symphony. After that he summoned the strength to record the work, and then made a written announcement of his resignation as chief conductor of the Berlin Philharmonic. It was the somewhat inglorious end of a great partnership which, strictly speaking, had begun in April 1938.

At the end of June Karajan traveled to the Swiss health spa of Leukerbad. Back in Salzburg he began rehearsing Verdi's *Un ballo in maschera* for the Summer Festival. On July 16, 1989 Herbert von Karajan received his last guests: Norio Ohga, the president of Sony, and Michael Schulhof, CEO of the Sony Corporation in America. Conversation revolved around Karajan's "musical legacy". Suddenly he asked for a glass of water. After drinking he slumped to the side, dead. On that July 16, 1989, Leonard Bernstein was conducting in Paris, and learned of Karajan's death in the middle of a concert. He interrupted the concert and asked the audience to stand in commemoration of "la mémoire d'un collègue, le grand maître Herbert von Karajan".

This time God did not interrupt.

1925 | Studio portrait of Ernst von Karajan, father of Herbert von Karajan.

1925 | Martha von Karajan, mother of Herbert von Karajan.

1915 | Wolfgang and Heribert Ritter von Karajan, pictured here with their housekeeper. During the 1920s, Heribert asked to be called Herbert.

1915 | Herbert von Karajan with his brother, Wolfgang.

1933 | Young Herbert at 24.

1939 | St Anton, Austria | Herbert von Karajan in the Tyrol mountains.

1938 | Herbert von Karajan drives his brand new BMW with his friend Edouard Hueber.

1939 | St Anton, Austria | Wolfgang
von Karajan, with friends Edouard
and Marie Hueber, and Herbert von
Karajan on the ski slopes.

1940 | Salzburg, Austria | In the mountains surrounding Salzburg.

Pages 30-31:
1940 | Aachen, Germany | Herbert von Karajan as a young conductor, after becoming Opernkapellmeister in this historical city in 1934. Less than a year later, he was assigned Generalmusik-
direktor. At the age of 27, he is Germany's youngest Musikdirektor.

January 1940 |
Promotional material
annnouncing an early
Deutsche Grammophon
recording of Herbert von
Karajan.

May 18, 1941 | Paris, France | The young Herbert von Karajan and the Berlin Opera to perform *Tristan et Isolde*, by Richard Wagner.

33

1942 | Although still young, Herbert von Karajan, is friends with composer Richard Strauss and Heinz Tietjen, general manager of the Berlin Opera. Karajan had already conducted two years earlier in the presence of the illustrious composer.

1943 | Portrait of the young conductor.

May 1941 | Paris | Germaine Lubin (1890-1979), a French soprano, with Herbert von Karajan.

Page 37: 1943 | Study of Herbert von Karajan's technique.

*Replié sur lui-même, attendant la première note, Karajan lève sa baguette...*

*Par des gestes très doux il contient encore la mélodie qui voudrait s'épanouir...*

*...et maintenant d'un mouvement libre et vaste, il la fait s'élever de toute sa puissance sonore.*

*Du regard, il dirige la grave cantilène qu'interprète un soliste.*

*De sa main gauche, il accentue gaiement l'étincelant scherzo.*

*Les cuivres, au fond, sont également conduits d'une main légère.*

*Il réussit à tirer de l'orchestre des nuances toujours nouvelles.*

*Toutes les forces sont déchaînées. Le chef d'orchestre s'abandonne à l'ivresse des sons.*

*D'un geste énergique, il assemble tous les instruments sur les dernières mesures de la symphonie.*

January 16, 1950 | Frankfurt, Germany | Herbert von Karajan with is musicians at the end of a performance.

1951 | Driving his sports car.

1951 | Italy | Herbert von Karajan with pianist Meyer and an unidentified guest.

1955 | New York, NY | Herbert von Karajan in contact with enthusiastic listeners during his first tour with the Berlin Philharmonic, which received him as its conductor for life shortly after Wilhelm Fürtwängler's death in 1954.

" The direction doesn't matter. Whether it's conducting, skiing or motor-racing, I simply want to be the best."

Herbert von Karajan, at 18.

# Herbert von KARAJAN
## THE DISTINGUISHED CONDUCTOR

**COLUMBIA**
*the finest name on record*

on

October 17.1955 | Autographed picture.

1956 | In concert.

1957 | Salzburg, Austria | During the Salzburg Easter Festival, where he acts as artistic director, Herbert von Karajan rehearses a scene from *Fidelio*, by Ludwig van Beethoven with German soprano Christel Goltz (1912 - ).

1957 | Salzburg, Austria | During the Salzburg Easter Festival, Herbert von Karajan rehearses a scene from *Fidelio*, by Ludwig van Beethoven, and shows the choir of the prisoners how to move.

1957 | Lucerne, Switzerland |
Herbert von Karajan on a speed-
boat on Léman Lake.

1957 | Lucerne, Switzerland | Herbert von Karajan with his 1954 Mercedes 300SL Gullwing.

1957 | Berlin | Herbert von Karajan conducts the Berlin Philharmonic.

1957 | Vienna, Austria | Herbert von Karajan in the Vienna Musikverein concert hall. This place is renowned for its "Salle dorée", where the Vienna Philharmonic performs each year the New Year's Concert for millions of spectators throughout the world.

51

October 16, 1958 | Herbert von Karajan with his wife Eliette Mouret, a young 17 year-old model, shortly after their wedding.

1959 | In one of his sports cars.

1960 | London, EMI Studios, Abbey Road | Herbert von Karajan during a recording session with the Berlin Philharmonic.

Pages 56-57:
1960 | Herbert von Karajan at work.

" After I learn a score, at the end I try and forget what I have seen, because seeing and hearing are two such different things."

Herbert von Karajan, explaining why he often conducted with closed eyes.

1960 | London, EMI Studios, Abbey Road | Herbert von Karajan during a recording session with the Berlin Philharmonic.

June 19, 1960 | Herbert von Karajan inaugurates construction of the new hall dedicated to hosting the Berlin Philharmonic.

June 19, 1960 | Eliette von Karajan and her husband during inauguration of the construction of the new hall dedicated to hosting the Berlin Philharmonic.

1962 | Together with Oskar Rothensteiner (left), Herbert von Karajan conducts and performs one of J.S. Bach's Brandenburg concertos.

1963 | Vienna | Herbert von Karajan during a press conference.

Pages 64-65:
1962 | Herbert von Karajan at work with Soviet pianist Sviatoslav Richter (1915 - 1997).

1962 | Karajan while conducting in near darkness.

January 24, 1963 | Milan | Herbert von Karajan in front of the Scala after rehearsing *La Bohème* by Puccini.

September 21, 1963 | Milan | Karajan in his car after rehearsing Verdi's Requiem Mass.

1963 | Herbert von Karajan during a rehersal.

1963 | Herbert von Karajan while rehearsing.

1964 | Saint Moritz | Birth of Arabella, Eliette and Herbert's second daughter. Arabella's godparents are the Berlin Philharmonic.

Summer 1964 | Herbert von Karajan with Isabella.

1965 | Salzburg | Herbert von Karajan during the Easter Festival, following a performance of *Boris Godounov* by Modeste Moussorgsky, with the Bulgarian bass singer Nicolaï Ghiaurov (1929-2004) and the Bosniac soprano Sena Jurinac (1921 - ).

1964 | Portrait of Herbert von Karajan.

1964 | The Karajan family in Saint-Moritz.

1964 | Eliette and Herbert von Karajan in Saint-Moritz.

1965 | In Salzburg.

1965 | Eliette Von Karajan shoots her husband with an 8mm camera.

1965 | Herbert von Karajan at work with Soviet pianist Sviatoslav Richter (1915 - 1997).

1965 | Herbert von Karajan in discussions with the set designer Guenther Schneider-Siemssen (1926 - ), who became famous through his unique use of stage lighting.

December 6, 1965 | Vienna |
Herbert von Karajan on the set
of *La Bohème*, filmed by his
own company, Cosmotel.

December 6, 1965 | Vienna | Herbert von Karajan on the set of *La Bohème*, with French director Henri-Georges Clouzot.

December 28, 1965 | Herbert von
Karajan on the Saint-Moritz slopes.

1965 | Herbert von Karajan films his concerts for television.

"I often listen to my colleagues. But I cannot accept a decision I disagree with. And I don't like compromising."

Herbert von Karajan

December 6, 1965 | Vienna | Herbert
von Karajan on the set of *La Bohème*,
filmed by his own company Cosmotel.

Pages 94-95:
1967 | Berlin | Herbert von Karajan and the Berlin Philharmonic while rehearsing in the Jesus Christ church.

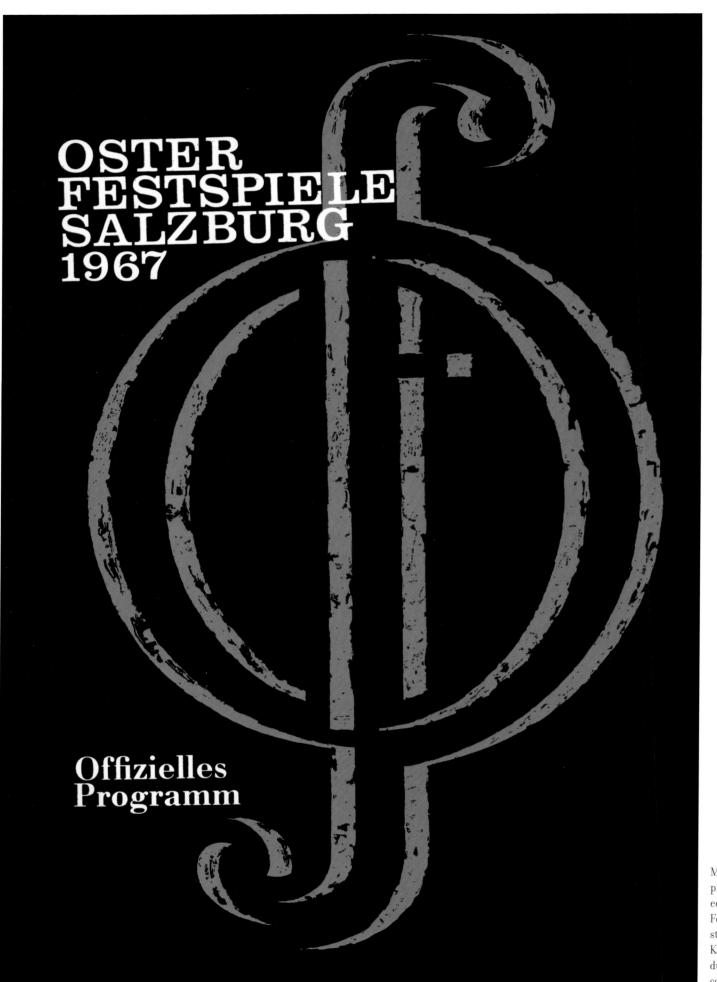

OSTER
FESTSPIELE
SALZBURG
1967

Offizielles
Programm

March 1967 | Cover of the program for the inaugural edition of the Easter Salzburg Festival. This festival was started by Herbert von Karajan to allow him to produce opera while keeping full control of performances.

March 1967 | Portrait excerpted from the program for the inaugural edition of the Easter Salzburg Festival.

May 23, 1967 | Rome | Herbert von Karajan conducts at the Vatican with Pope Paul VI among the attendees.

May 23, 1967 | Rome | After his performance, Herbert von Karajan is introduced to Pope Paul VI in the Palazzo Pio auditorium.

March 1967 | Eliette and Herbert von Karajan during the inaugural edition of the Salzburg Easter Festival.

1969 | Herbert von Karajan rehearses with Russian cellist Mstislav Rostropovitch (1927-2007).

1967 | Herbert von Karajan
during a concert
brodcasted on television.

1967 | Vienna | Herbert von Karajan during the recording of Bizet's *Carmen*, with the Vienna Philharmonic and the Vienna State Opera Choir.

1968 | Herbert von Karajan is very involved in every technical aspect of his videorecordings.

1968 | Vienna | Herbert von Karajan with family.

1967 | Saint-Tropez | Herbert von Karajan on holiday.

1968 | Herbert von Karajan stepping out of one of his many automobiles.

1968 | Eliette and Herbert von Karajan.

1968 | Herbert von Karajan at the music stand.

1968 | Herbert von Karajan during a rehearsal.

1967 | Vienna | Herbert von Karajan is actively involved in directing Bizet's *Carmen* with the Vienna Philharmonic and the Vienna State Opera Choir.

1968 | Herbert von Karajan during a rehearsal.

8478

1968 | Herbert von Karajan rehearsing.

1969 | Herbert von Karajan rehearsing.

1969 | Paris | Herbert von Karajan rehearses with German pianist and conductor Justus Franz (1944 −), and German pianist then conductor Christoph Eschenbach (1940 −), a longtime Karajan protégé.

1969 | An intimate moment with Eliette.

Page 117:
1969 | Saint-Moritz | Herbert von Karajan works in his chalet.

116

1969 | Herbert von Karajan with
American composer and writer
Nicolas Nabokov (1903-1978),
cousin of Vladimir Nabokov
(1899-1977).

February 3, 1969 | Herbert von Karajan inspects a mockup of the forthcoming second major concert hall to be built in Munich, with project head Josef Schorghuber.

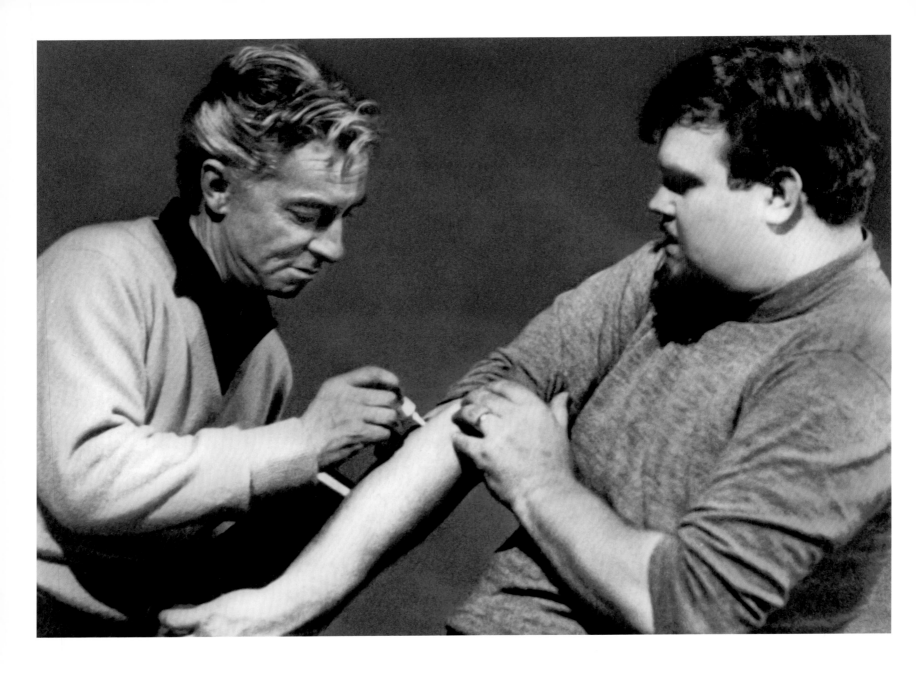

April 2, 1969 | During a reherasal of the *Rhinegold* by Richard Wagner, to be performed during the Salzburg Festival, Herbert von Karajan attends to the wound of the Finish bass singer Martti Talvela (1935-1989), who plays Fasold.

Page 121:
1969 | Herbert von Karajan during a rehearsal.

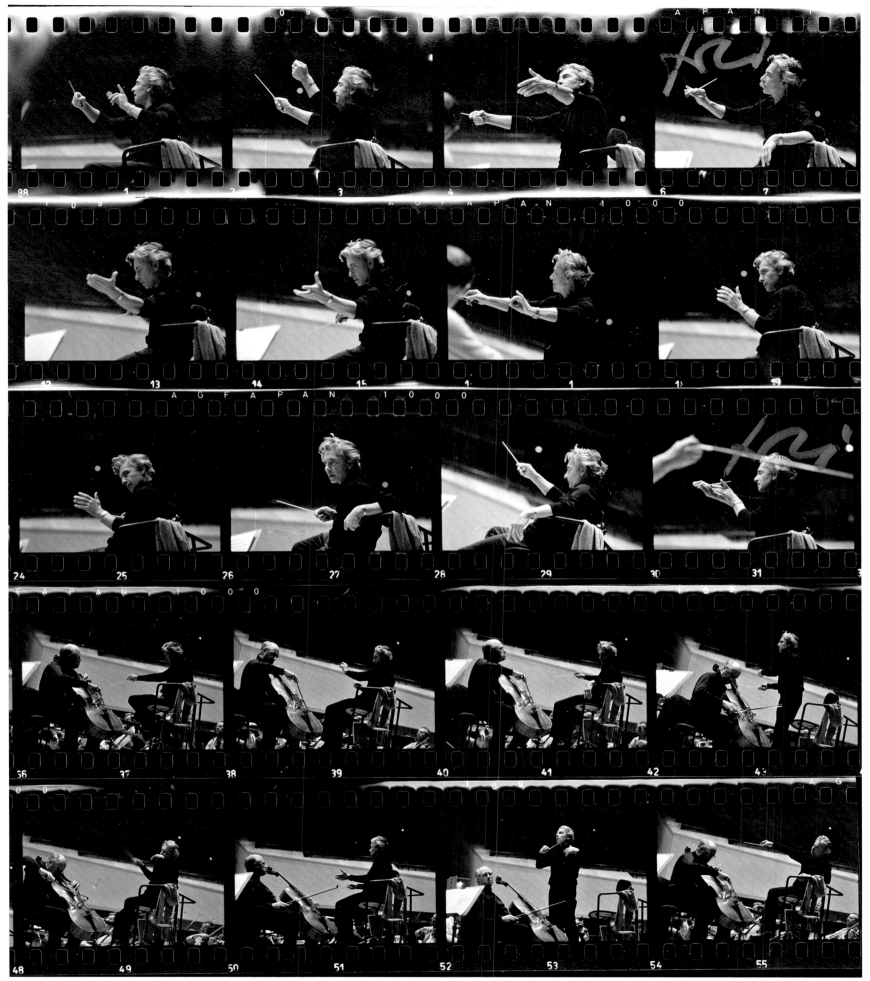

# " Each concert is a mystical experience. "

Herbert von Karajan

Approx. 1970 | Herbert von Karajan
and Spanish tenor José Carerras
(1946 – ) rehearse Verdi's *Aida*.

Pages 126-127:
1971 | The Herbert von Karajan technique.

1971 | The Herbert von Karajan technique.

" The study of the history of music and the hearing of masterworks of different epochs will quickly cure you of vanity and self-adoration."

Robert Schumann (1810-1856)

BILDPLATTE · VIDEO DISC

1971 | Herbert von Karajan during the introduction of the vidéo-disc format to the press.

Pages 130 to 133:
1972 | Backstage with Herbert von Karajan.

1973 | Herbert von Karajan in a recording studio.

1973 | Debating with colleagues.

1973 | Eliette and Herbert von Karajan.

1974 | Herbert von Karajan
tapes a concert for television.

" Playing music is like creating a bridge with a composer long gone, like following his steps and seeing him at work."

Hubert Reeves, Canadian astrophysicist.

1975 | Herbert von Karajan with
German baritone Dietrich
Fischer-Dieskau (1925—).

1975 | Herbert von Karajan in Berlin.

1976 | Herbert von Karajan receiving an ovation from his public.

April 1978 | Vienna | Herbert von Karajan reads the score in the control room of the Sofiensaal studio during the recording of *The Marriage of Figaro* by W. A. Mozart.

April 1978 | Vienna | Herbert von Karajan while recording *The Marriage of Figaro*.

1978 | Herbert von Karajan listens carefully to one of his studio recordings.

1979 | Herbert von Karajan in studio with German violinist Anne-Sophie Mutter and American cellist Yo-Yo Ma.

# "Without music, life would be a mistake."

Friedrich Nietzsche

Pages 149 to 151:
1978 | Münich | Herbert von Karajan on the set of the *Rhinegold* movie, with Jeannine Altmeyer, Brigitte Fassbaender and Peter Schreier. This film was shot entirely in studio under the artistic supervision of the great conductor.

" If I tell the Berliners to step forward, they do it. If I tell the Viennese to step forward, they do it. But then they ask why."

Herbert von Karajan, explaining why he preferred conducting the Berlin Philharmonic to the Vienna Philharmonic.

Approx. 1980 | Herbert von Karajan during a rehearsal.

1980 | Courchevel, France | Herbert von Karajan with young violinist Anne-Sophie Mutter.

1980 | Herbert von Karajan with German tenor Peter Hoffmann (1944 – ).

Pages 156 to 159:
1980 | Highlights from the Karajan conducting style.

"I cannot teach you to conduct, but I can show you how to rehearse in such a way that, when you come to the concert itself, you will barely need to conduct."

Herbert von Karajan

1981 | Herbert von Karajan in Berlin.

April 15, 1981 | Salzburg | Herbert von Karajan sits at the press conference for the international introduction of the CD audio format, next to Sony chairman Akio Morita, during the Salzburg Easter Festival.

1981 | In conversation with Kurt Masur, then head of the Gewandhausorchester Leipzig.

February 19, 1983 | German soprano Elisabeth Schwarzkopf (1915-2006) offers Herbert von Karajan a restrospective album about his career as a conductor.

1983 | Herbert von Karajan listens to one of his recordings.

" The art of conducting consists in knowing when to stop conducting to let the orchestra play. "

Herbert von Karajan

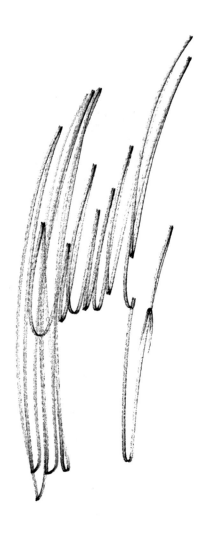

1985 | Herbert von Karajan as seen by photographer Tom Baziroff.

1986 | Herbert von Karajan with
Anne-Sophie Mutter.

1984 | During the Salzburg Easter Festival.

1985 | Herbert von Karajan in concert.

March 26, 1986 | Herbert von Karajan with Akio Morita announcing plans for a CD plant in Anif, near Salzburg.

1984 | Salzburg | Herbert von Karajan follows closely the editing of his recordings.

"Due to the single fact that I have met and worked with Herbert von Karajan, I consider myself as an extremely lucky person.

"A man who became a living legend and remained one during the last several decades of his life; whose name became a personification of the notion "conductor", a synonym of this word for millions of people; one of the very few so-called "universal" musicians who reached towering heights in Mozart and Tchaikovsky, Wagner and Shostakovich, Bruckner and Strauss. After Karajan's performance of Strauss' Jupiter Symphony with the Berlin Philharmonic in Moscow in early 1960s, one respectable Russian musician said: *But in fact there was no conductor, no orchestra – only Mozart was there!*".

"*An artist's approval should be more important for you than a whole crowd's recognition*" Schumann wrote in his *Life Rules for Musicians*. Probably the most gratifying approval I've ever received in my life, the one I will most cherish as long as I live, is when I met Herbert von Karajan for the first time, played for him – and after finishing playing Chopin's *Fantaisie in F-Minor*, I saw him wiping his eyes with a handkerchief. At the end of that meeting, Mrs. von Karajan, who was there too, said:"*I have been married to my husband for thirty years and have never seen him so moved!*"

"No doubt for a single such moment that life is worth living."

Evgeny Kissin, 2007

1987 | Herbert von Karajan with Russian pianist Evgeny Kissin (1971 –).

1987 | Herbert von
Karajan in action.

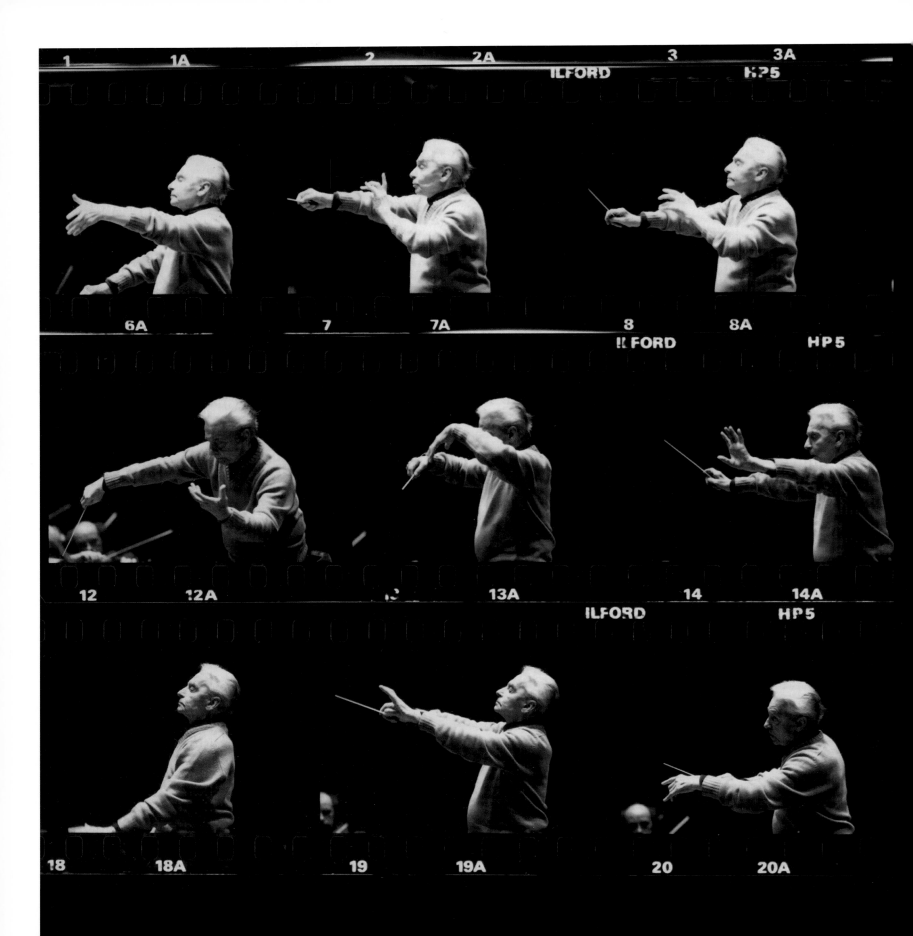

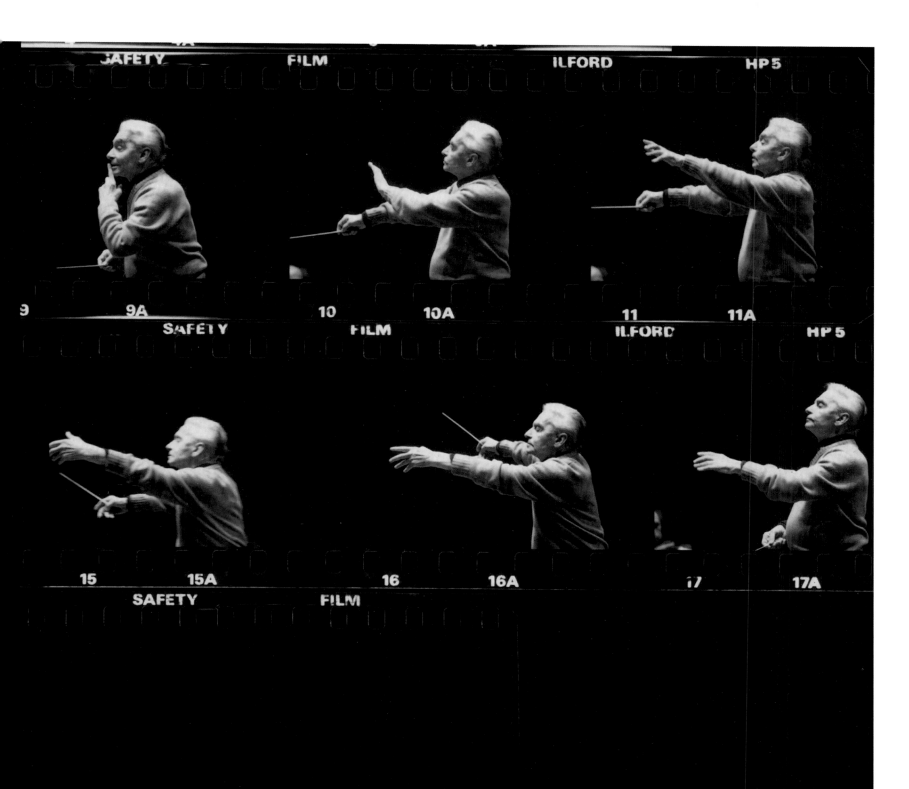

SAFETY FILM ILFORD HP 5

9    9A    10    10A    11    11A

SAFETY FILM ILFORD HP 5

15    15A    16    16A    17    17A

SAFETY FILM

21    21A    22    22A

Pages 184–185:
April 20, 1989 | The last recording session of Herbert von Karajan: Bruckner's Symphony No. 7.

Page 186:
Herbert von Karajan in 1987.

Page 187:
1989 | Herbert von Karajan
rehearses with Italian tenor
Luciano Pavarotti (1935 - 2007).

1989 | An intimate moment between Herbert and Eliette during the Salzburg Easter Festival.

1989 | Herbert von Karajan shortly before his death. This is the last photograph taken by Siegfried Lauterwasser.

# DISCOGRAPHY

1943 | Johannes Brahms | Symphony No. 1, Amsterdam Concertgebouw Orchestra
1946 | Ludwig van Beethoven | Symphony No. 8, Vienna Philharmonic
1947 | Ludwig van Beethoven | Symphony No. 9, Vienna Philharmonic
1947 | Johannes Brahms | Ein deutsches Requiem, Vienna Philharmonic
1948 | Robert Schumann | Piano concerto, Philharmonia Orchestra, Dinu Lipatti
1949 | Giuseppe Verdi | Requiem Mass, Vienna Philharmonic

1951 | Richard Strauss | Don Juan, Philharmonia Orchestra
1952 | Wolfgang A. Mozart | Le nozze di Figaro, Philharmonia Orchestra
1952 | Jean Sibelius | Symphony No. 5, Philharmonia Orchestra
1953 | Belá Bartók | Concerto for orchestra, Philharmonia Orchestra
1953 | Jean Sibelius | Symphony No. 4, Philharmonia Orchestra
1954 | Wolfgang A. Mozart | Così fan tutte, Philharmonia Orchestra
1954 | Richard Strauss | Ariadne auf Naxos, Philharmonia Orchestra
1955 | Giacomo Puccini | Madame Butterfly, Orchestra of la Scala, Milan
1955 | Jean Sibelius | Symphony No. 6 and No. 7, Philharmonia Orchestra
1956 | Richard Strauss | The Knight of he Rose, Philharmonia Orchestra
1956 | Giuseppe Verdi | Il Trovatore, Orchestra of la Scala, Milan
1956 | Giuseppe Verdi | Falstaff, Philharmonia Orchestra
1959 | Giuseppe Verdi | Aida, Vienna Philharmonic

1960 | Richard Strauss | Don Juan, Till Eulenspiegel, Vienna Philharmonic
1960 | Richard Strauss | Le Chevalier à la Rose, Vienna Philharmonic
1961 | Giuseppe Verdi | Othello, Vienna Philharmonic
1962 | Giacomo Puccini | Tosca, Vienna Philharmonic
1962 | Ludwig van Beethoven | Symphonies No. 1 to 9, Berlin Philharmonic
1963 | Richard Wagner | Tannhäuser, Vienna Philharmonic
1964 | Johannes Brahms | Symphonys No.1 à 4, Berlin Philharmonic
1964 | Richard Strauss | Elektra, Vienna Philharmonic
1965 | Jean Sibelius | Symphony No. 5, Berlin Philharmonic
1966 | Dmitri Shostakovitch | Symphony No. 10, Berlin Philharmonic
1966 | Richard Wagner | The Valkyrie, Berlin Philharmonic
1967 | Richard Wagner | The Rhinegold, Berlin Philharmonic
1968 | Richard Wagner | Siegfried, Berlin Philharmonic
1969 | Richard Wagner | Twilight of the Gods, Berlin Philharmonic
1969 | Ludwig van Beethoven | Triple concerto, Berlin Philharmonic
1969 | Arthur Honegger | Symphony No. 3, Berlin Philharmonic

1970 | Richard Wagner | The Mastersingers of Nuremberg, Saxon State Orchestra, Dresden
1970 | Ludwig van Beethoven | Fidelio, Berlin Philharmonic
1972 | Giuseppe Verdi | Requiem Mass, Berlin Philharmonic
1972 | Richard Wagner | Tristan and Isolde, Berlin Philharmonic
1972 | Giacomo Puccini | La Bohème, Berlin Philharmonic
1973 | Gustav Mahler | Symphony No. 5, Berlin Philharmonic
1973 | Johann Sebastian Bach | Mass in h-moll, Berlin Philharmonic
1974 | Richard Strauss | Don Juan, Thus spoke Zarathustra, Berlin Philharmonic
1974 | Richard Wagner | Lohengrin, Berlin Philharmonic
1976 | Anton Bruckner | Symphonies No. 1 to 9, Berlin Philharmonic
1977 | Richard Strauss | Salomé, Vienna Philharmonic
1978 | Johannes Brahms | Symphonies No. 1 to 4, Berlin Philharmonic
1978 | Giuseppe Verdi | Don Carlo, Berlin Philharmonic

1978 | Claude Debussy | Pelleas and Mélisande, Berlin Philharmonic
1978 | Gustav Mahler | Symphony No. 6, Berlin Philharmonic
1979 | Giacomo Puccini | Tosca, Berlin Philharmonic

1980 | Wolfgang A. Mozart | The Magic Flute, Berlin Philharmonic
1980 | Giuseppe Verdi | Falstaff, Vienna Philharmonic
1981 | Richard Wagner | Parsifal, Berlin Philharmonic
1982 | Georges Bizet | Carmen, Berlin Philharmonic
1985 | Wolfgang A. Mozart | Don Giovanni, Berlin Philharmonic
1986 | Wolfgang A. Mozart | Requiem, Vienna Philharmonic
1988 | Anton Bruckner | Symphony No. 8, Berlin Philharmonic
1989 | Anton Bruckner | Symphony No. 7, Vienna Philharmonic

# PHOTO CREDITS

# ACKNOWLEDGMENTS

*"Je dédie ce livre à Anne Verlhac, sans laquelle tout cela ne serait pas."*
This work is dedicated to Anne Verlhac, without whom all this could not exist.

Pierre-Henri Verlhac

The editor would like to thank the following people, in alphabetical order:

Barbara Diesner, Evgeny Kissin, Alexander Lauterwasser, Linda Perkins.